FOUNDATIONS OF MUSIC EDUCATION SERIES
Allen P. Britton, Editor

Prentice-Hall International, Inc., *London*
Prentice-Hall of Australia, Pty. Ltd., *Sydney*
Prentice-Hall of Canada, Ltd., *Toronto*
Prentice-Hall of India Private Ltd., *New Delhi*
Prentice-Hall of Japan, Inc., *Tokyo*

Teaching
Rhythm and Using
Classroom Instruments

Teaching Rhythm and Using Classroom Instruments

MARGUERITE V. HOOD

Professor of Music
School of Music
The University of Michigan

PRENTICE-HALL, INC., *Englewood Cliffs, New Jersey*

© 1970 by Prentice-Hall, Inc., Englewood Cliffs, New Jersey

Current printing (last digit)
10 9 8 7 6 5 4 3 2 1

Library of Congress Catalog Card Number: 73-95750

Printed in the United States of America

C-13-894089-4
P-13-894063-0

Foreword

The practical aim of the Foundations of Music Education Series is to provide music educators with a unified but highly flexible and completely authoritative treatment of the most important professional concerns. Individual books of the series may be combined in various ways to form complete textbooks for the wide variety of courses in music education offered by colleges and universities across the nation. On the other hand, each volume has been designed to stand alone as a definitive treatment of its particular subject area.

The pedagogical aim of the series is to present practical and proven techniques of successful teaching in compact and readable form for both college students preparing to teach and experienced teachers constantly searching for more efficient ways of thinking and teaching. The highest musical ideals must be accompanied by the greatest amount of practical common sense if music instruction is to be most successful.

The aesthetic aim of the series is to emphasize the purely musical values that must be realized in any program of music instruction if that program is to achieve ends worthy of the time and effort required to carry it on. In short, each of these works assumes first of all that music must be true to itself if it is to continue to hold a respected place in

American education. The most telling criticisms made of the school music program in recent years, almost all of which have dealt largely with alleged aesthetic failings, have written this lesson in letters large enough for all to read.

Last, having pointed out the unifying concepts that underlie the works in this series, it is perhaps equally important to emphasize that each of the authors has written the book that he wanted to write, the book that he believed would be of most value to the profession. The series encompasses the individual convictions of a great variety of the most highly competent and experienced music educators. On their behalf as well as on my own, may I express the hope that it will contribute in a practical way to the improvement of music teaching.

ALLEN P. BRITTON

EDITOR

Preface

The title of this book may give the impression that the material included in it deals with two entirely different and separate areas of elementary school music teaching. Further thought and examination, however, will show that there are few (if any) areas in the teaching of rhythm which cannot be helped and made considerably easier and more enjoyable for both teacher and children through the use of some of the classroom instruments.

Also, although only a few of the classroom instruments are specifically rhythm instruments, *all* of them require a feeling for rhythm pulsation and some skill in responding to it, in order to play them successfully, whatever their type may be. The two subjects included in the title are not unrelated.

This book is directed to teachers of elementary school music, both those who are in college, in music education classes or directed teaching of music, and those who are currently active in the professional teaching field. It is planned for use by both music specialists and general classroom teachers.

All the details about beginning instruction on each of the instruments discussed are not given here. Instead, there is included instruction in only the most basic skills in using the instruments in the general classroom, together with a variety of musical materials and suggested activities. Most teachers will wish to make considerable use of the bibliographies which include listings of more detailed methods of instruction, suggested songs from the familiar elementary school series books, special collections of music, and recordings, all of which are available for enriching the various individual areas of experience.

The excitement of learning new ideas and of making music in new and different ways can stimulate a child to identify himself with an active, on-going experience in music. Such individual and group participation can have great importance in meeting the needs of children in the world of today.

Marguerite V. Hood

Contents

PART TWO

USING CLASSROOM INSTRUMENTS
IN THE GENERAL MUSIC PROGRAM

4 INTRODUCTION   49

5 TRADITIONAL RHYTHM
INSTRUMENTS IN THE CLASSROOM   54

6 FOLK AND NATIONAL
RHYTHM PERCUSSION INSTRUMENTS   63

7 TUNED BAR INSTRUMENTS
AND KEYBOARD INSTRUMENTS   85

PART I

TEACHING RHYTHM
IN THE
ELEMENTARY SCHOOL

1

Introduction

Probably no term used in speaking or writing about music has been recognized by as many different definitions as has *rhythm.* Each definition seems to have been tailored by its creator to fit his own professional needs, be he performer, conductor, musicologist, teacher, composer, or unschooled amateur. A wide variety of statements similar to the following abound: Rhythm is the lifebeat of music . . . . Rhythm is the organization of music into patterns of accented and unaccented sounds . . . . The term *rhythm* covers all that has to do with varying lengths of sounds in music . . . . These and other statements about rhythm, even when they are basically in agreement, frequently differ so widely in emphasis as to give rise to heated controversy.

Exact definitions of terms in music are not always needed by either amateurs or professionals, but the fact that there is such a diversity of ideas regarding the subject may help to explain the necessity for a wide variety of activity in teaching rhythm to children. Regardless of the definition accepted, rhythm exists as a basic element in music, an element that has many facets. Some of these facets are obvious and are brought into use by natural, almost instinctive response. Others make demands in skill and understanding that require a planned and structured learning process.

In considering the teaching of rhythm, it is important to recognize, along with the multiplicity of areas in rhythm itself, the fact that the children in the classes being taught develop as individuals and not uniformly in groups. And they learn in many different ways and at varying speeds. To meet the needs of individual children as they learn and to provide a rich and diversified experience with the many facets of rhythm at every school level, these chapters in Part 1 include the following subjects:

1. Ways of learning to make response to the rhythm of music and to feel the joy of "keeping time" through bodily activity, whether by simple physical movement, by playing a rhythm instrument, or by participating in a game or dance.
2. Ways of learning to recognize both simple rhythm patterns and rhythms composed of notes of various lengths by means of the combined activities of listening to them and moving to them.
3. Ways of developing an intelligent understanding of the different elements of rhythm notation and of acquiring such skill in the use of this notation as is needed to provide for varying individual interests in singing, playing, and listening to the rich literature of music that is available to today's boys and girls—children's songs, folk, traditional, and popular music, and composed music, including that of the twentieth century.

GENERAL SUGGESTIONS
FOR TEACHERS

1. Not all children enjoy or have success with all the activities suggested in each section that follows. Variety in approach and experience will help to meet individual needs and interests.
2. Many of the activities suggested here are usable at all age levels, with small children and also with older boys and girls. Some are too complex for most groups of small children. It is suggested that, where experiences that gradually increase in difficulty are concerned, any group of children should participate in the activities as long as they are easily within the ability of most of the children. The possible limits of the accomplishments of boys and girls depend more upon previous experience and immediate interests than upon grade level.
3. Teachers of both vocal and instrumental music in the elementary schools should recognize the fact that if boys and girls are to be helped to reach the point where they enjoy music and can use it by playing or singing for their own immediate and continuing pleasure,

the experiences of *moving to music,* and of *learning to hear and then respond to rhythms* are essential preliminaries to the successful use of rhythmic notation.

4. The time to teach each of the items included here is when it is needed for successful independent music making, regardless of the age level.

5. The choice of music for the initial presentation of a new idea is extremely important. Most of the musical materials included in these chapters or suggested from various school music books are very simply-constructed examples. New ideas are usually introduced through music that is already familiar. Anything that can be easily understood and successfully used will help teach itself. The difficulties sometimes experienced in learning to use music notation may result from the fact that the music used is not suitable. When a new idea is being brought into play, the understanding of it may be confused by the presence of an assortment of strange and seemingly complex problems in the musical material. This is particularly true of the learning of rhythmic concepts. The choice of musical examples for introductory lessons is of the greatest importance, not only to the immediate success and enjoyment of the class, but also to the development of skill and of the initiative boys and girls have to use any music that interests them.

A FEW GENERAL SOURCES ON TEACHING RHYTHM

Additional sources are listed in connection with the sections on certain phases of rhythm teaching. The teachers' manuals for the various elementary school music series also include valuable material on the subject of teaching rhythm. (See page 129.)

Film

Rhythmic Rounds, Edna Doll and Mary Jarman Nelson. Fort Worth, Texas: Rhythm Band Inc.

Books

Ellison, Alfred, *Music with Children.* New York: McGraw-Hill Book Company, 1959.

Garretson, Robert L., *Music in Childhood Education.* New York: Appleton-Century-Crofts, 1966.

Gary, Charles L. (ed.), *The Study of Music in the Elementary School.* Washington, D.C.: Music Educators National Conference, 1967.

Gray, Vera, and Rachel Percival, *Music, Movement, and Mime.* New York: Oxford Publishing Comany, Inc., 1965. Records: *Listen, Move, and Dance,* Vols. I and II, Capitol records H-21006 and H-21007.

Hood, Marguerite V., and E. J. Schultz, *Learning Music Through Rhythm.* Boston: Ginn and Company, 1949.

Nye, Robert E., and Bjornar Bergethon, *Basic Music: An Activities Approach to Functional Musicianship* (3rd ed.). Englewood Cliffs, N.J.: Prentice-Hall, Inc., 1968.

Nye, Robert E. and Vernice T. Nye, *Music in the Elementary School* (3rd ed.). Englewood Cliffs, N.J.: Prentice-Hall, Inc., 1970.

Runkle, Aleta, and Mary LeBow Eriksen, *Music for Today's Boys and Girls.* Boston: Allyn & Bacon, 1966.

Slind, Lloyd H., and D. Evan Davis, *Bringing Music To Children.* New York: Harper & Row, Publishers, 1964.

Swanson, Bessie R., *Music in the Education of Children* (3rd ed.). Belmont, Calif.: Wadsworth Publishing Company, Inc., 1969.

2

Moving

to Music

The first basic experiences boys and girls of all grade levels need in order to develop understanding and skill with rhythm are those that lead them as individuals to recognize and feel the rhythmic swing and pulsations in music and to respond to them with physical movement. The activities included in this chapter will contribute to this development. They include the following types of experiences, each of which makes important contributions to the growth of rhythmic awareness and skill: experiences in which free bodily movement is used; imitative and dramatic rhythmic activities; rhythmic movement through games and dances; and playing rhythm instruments.

FREE BODILY MOVEMENT

The first thing any child must learn in order to develop an understanding of rhythm is to feel the swing and the pulsations in the music and to respond to them by moving his body. Every child has his own personal rhythm, which he uses in bodily movements like walking, running, or skipping. Many children, however, have not yet discovered that music has a swing and a beat and that, by adjusting their movements in speed and accent, they can fit these movements to the rhythm of the music. This type of activity is important at every level of growth and should not be limited to the kindergarten.

Suggested Activities

Most of the following activities require a large amount of space if the movements are to be free and unhampered.

1. *Small children.* Large, free movements that use the whole body: hopping, skipping, running, creeping on the floor, waving strips of crepe paper or scarfs, bouncing balls.
2. *Older children.* Marching, clapping, swinging arms, bending, swaying, tapping fingers, echo clapping. A game, "Musical Follow the Leader," can be played with the teacher or a student as the leader, and with a variety of movements. This can be done sometimes without even having the children move from their places. For echo clapping, see page 134.

Sources:
Music for Free
Rhythmic Activity

The steady rhythmic beat of a drum or other percussion instrument is suitable for walking, skipping, and other types of physical movement done rhythmically. Recorded music and piano music are usable when they are at a speed that is comfortable for the activity concerned. The following list includes some of the many available books and recordings that can provide music and that also frequently include teaching suggestions.

Books

Buttolph, Edna G., *Music Is Motion.* Cincinnati: Willis Music Co., 1951.

Doll, Edna and Mary Jarman Nelson, *Rhythms Today!* Morristown, N.J.: Silver Burdett Company, 1965. Book and records.

Evans, Ruth, *40 Basic Rhythms for Children.* Putnam, Conn.: U.S. Textbook Co., 1958. Records: *Rhythms for Children.* Springfield, Mass.: The Children's World, Inc., CW 1001, CW 1002.

Hood, Marguerite V., and E. J. Schultz, *Learning Music Through Rhythm.* Boston: Ginn and Company, 1949.

Saffran, Rosanna B., *Creative Rhythms*. New York: Holt, Rinehart & Winston, Inc., 1963.

Records

Basic Rhythmic Activities. Los Angeles: Children's Music Center.
Rhythm Is Fun. Glendale, Calif.: Bowmar Records, Inc.
Things to Do. New York: Young People's Records, The Greystone Corp.

IMITATIVE AND DRAMATIC ACTIVITY

Many children discover how to respond to a musical rhythm through a dramatic type of activity in which they imitate a movement such as that of another human being, an imaginary being, a familiar animal or something in nature. "Props" are often important in these activities. A child who is too shy to participate freely in basic rhythmic activity frequently loses his timidity when he pretends to be someone else, particularly if he uses a "prop" like a scarf, a sash, or a hat when he enacts a dramatic part.

Some Suggested Types of Imitative or Dramatic Musical Activity

1. *Small Children*

   a. People, their activities and characteristics: shoemaker, old man, mother and baby, skier, carpenter, ballet dancer.
   b. Mechanical world: jet plane, train, pile driver.
   c. Nature: leaves in the wind, snowflakes falling, trees swaying.
   d. Animals and birds: horse, elephant, rabbit, kangaroo.
   e. Imaginary beings: elf, giant, fairy.
   f. Toys: walking doll, toy soldier, rag doll.
   g. Stories or familiar situations: market, fair, circus.

2. *Older Children*

   a. Mechanical movements: factory machinery, wheels, pistons, hammers.
   b. Human activity: work songs (sea chanteys and songs of lumberjacks, voyageurs, cowboys, railroad builders); orchestra conductor; traffic policeman.
   c. Story dramatization: rhythmic enactment of ballads, stories, and folk tales such as that of Paul Bunyan.

MY OLD HAMMER

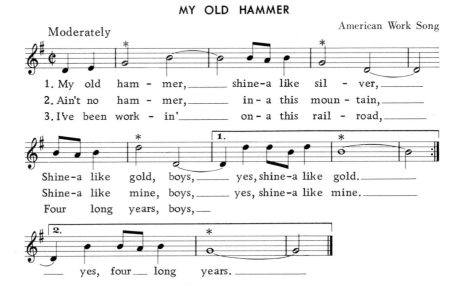

1. My old ham - mer,_____ shine-a like sil - ver,_____
2. Ain't no ham - mer,_____ in - a this moun - tain,_____
3. I've been work - in'_____ on - a this rail - road,_____

Shine-a like gold, boys,_____ yes, shine-a like gold._____
Shine-a like mine, boys,_____ yes, shine-a like mine._____
Four long years, boys,___

___ yes, four___ long years. _____

From *Growing With Music,* Book 5, by Harry R. Wilson, *et al.,* p. 130. © 1966 by Prentice-Hall, Inc., Englewood Cliffs, N.J. Reprinted with permission.

Since the sledgehammer is extremely heavy and difficult to lift, it would probably be struck on alternate measures as marked by*.

Sources:
Music for Imitative
and Dramatic Activity

Books

Andrews, Gladys, *Creative Rhythmic Movement for Children.* Englewood Cliffs, N.J.: Prentice-Hall, Inc., 1954.

Bampton, Ruth, *Come and Play.* New York: Mills Music, Inc., 1948.

Doll, Edna, and Mary Jarman Nelson, *Rhythms Today!* Book and records. Morristown, N.J.: Silver Burdett Company, 1965.

Evans, Ruth, *40 Basic Rhythms for Children.* Putnam, Conn.: U.S. Textbook Co., 1958. Records: *Rhythms for Children.* Springfield, Mass.: The Children's World, Inc., CW 1001, CW 1002.

Monsour, Sally, Marilyn C. Cohen, and Patricia E. Lindell, *Rhythm in Music and Dance for Children.* Belmont, Calif.: Wadsworth Publishing Company, Inc., 1966.

Tobitt, Janet, and Alice White, *Dramatized Ballads.* New York: E. P. Dutton & Co., Inc., 1937. Also, *The Saucy Sailor,* same authors and publisher, 1940.

White, Florence, and Kazuo Akiyama, *Children's Songs from Japan.* New York: Edward B. Marks Music Corporation, 1960.

Records

Imitative or dramatic activity requires music with a rhythm suitable for the movements to be made. By listening to music available to them on records, children soon learn to select the sounds and rhythms best suited to each type of rhythmic activity. Some examples of available recordings:

Adventures in Music. Albums for grades 1 to 6. RCA Victor.

"(The) Circus Comes to Town" from *Tom Glazer Sings.* Young People's Records, 7002.

Dance a Story About Balloons. Record and book. Also in *The Magic of Music, 3.* Ginn and Company.

"Hurricane" from *Rhythms Today!* (See listing above.)

"Our Furry Friends." Record for *The Magic of Music, Kindergarten.*

(The) Rhythm Program, Vols. I–VI. *RCA Victor Record Library for Elementary Schools.*

"Steel Foundry," Alexander Mossolov, from *Sounds of New Music.* Ethnic Folkways, FX6160.

"Under the Big Top," Herbert Donaldson, from *Animals and Circus.* Bowmar Orchestral Library No. 51.

Elementary Music Series Books

Most school song books include a variety of song material suitable for dramatic activity. Here are some examples: "The Bunny Song," *Growing With Music,* Book 2; "Hammer Man," *Making Music Your Own,* Book 5; "Six Little Ducks," *The Magic of Music,* Book 2; "Grasshoppers Three," *This Is Music,* Book 1; "Blow the Man Down," *Discovering Music Together,* Book 4; "Canoe Song," *Exploring Music,* Book 3; "Singin' Johnny," *Studying Music* (*Music for Young Americans,* Book 6).

GAMES AND DANCES

Folk and traditional games and dances, including singing games, can provide experience with many different types of rhythmic movement. In addition, particularly in folk dances, participation provides a valuable source of social activity and a considerable fund of international interest and understanding.

Teaching
Games and Dances

In presenting singing games, it is usually wise to teach the song first, adding the movements later. When available, a recorded or piano accompaniment should be used with a game. Boys and girls should be encouraged to sing lightly. Both singing and dancing require breath and energy, and strained, harsh voices can be the result of singing during strenuous physical activity. The best arrangement is to have part of the group furnish the singing accompaniment while the others dance. When children have learned a few traditional games and dances and have thus acquired a basic vocabulary of movement patterns, they can begin to create original dances to fit some of the songs they sing or the music they hear.

1. *Games for small children.* Games and dances that use large movements and that include repetition are especially suitable for use by small children. Here is an example:

DANCE WITH ME

Words by G. E. Price
German Folk Tune

Come, my friend, and dance with me,   It is eas-y,   you will see.

One step back,   one step out,   Then you twirl your-self a-bout.

From *Growing With Music, Book* 1, p. 19. © Prentice-Hall, Inc., 1966.

The children form two lines with the boys in one line facing the girls in the other. The lines should be about eight steps apart.
Verses. The boys and girls walk toward each other (four steps) during the first two measures. They take four steps back during the next two measures.
Refrain. Follow the directions given in the text.

2. *Games for older children.* There are many folk games and dances that require the skill and experience that older boys and girls have and are of interest to them. Included are some of the popular clapping games, marching games, and square dances. Here is a game these children enjoy.

HORA DANCE SONG

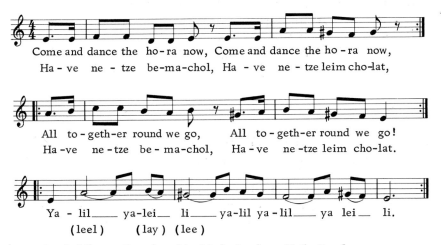

Come and dance the ho-ra now, Come and dance the ho-ra now,
Ha - ve ne - tze be-ma-chol, Ha - ve ne - tze leim cho-lat,

All to - geth-er round we go,   All to - geth-er round we go!
Ha -ve ne - tze be - ma-chol,   Ha - ve ne -tze leim cho-lat.

Ya - lil____ ya-lei__ li____ ya-lil ya - lil____ ya lei __ li.
(leel)   (lay) (lee)

Israeli folksong. Contributed by Moshe Jacobson, Haifa, Israel.

Everyone stands in a circle facing the center; hands rest on shoulders of those to either side. Dance steps:

a. Step, step, step. (Step to the right with the right foot; step to the right with the left foot, putting it down behind the right foot; step to the right with the right foot.)

b. Hop-kick, hop-kick. (Hop on the right foot, kicking the left foot in front of the right; hop on the left foot, kicking the right foot in front of the left.)

These steps are repeated continually, over and over again. At first the song and dance are slow, but gradually the speed is increased until the dancers are whirling rapidly. Although the dance is very strenuous, people in Israel often dance it for long periods without stopping.

Sources:
Music for
Games and Dances

Collections of Games and Dances

Latchaw, Marjorie, *A Pocket Guide of Games and Rhythms for the Elementary School.* Englewood Cliffs, N.J.: Prentice-Hall, Inc., 1956.

Pitcher, Gladys, *Playtime in Song.* New York: M. Witmark and Sons, 1960.

Rohrbough, Lynn, *Play Party Book*. Delaware, Ohio: Cooperative Recreation Service, 1940.

Tobitt, Janet, *Promenade All*. New York: Plymouth Music Co., Inc., 1947.

White, Florence, and Kazuo Akiyama, *Children's Songs from Japan*. New York: Edward B. Marks Music Corporation, 1960.

Wiseman, Herbert, and Sydney Northcote, *The Clarendon Books of Singing Games*, Books 1 and 2. New York: Oxford University Press, Inc., 1957.

Records

Play Party Games. Vols. 1 and 2. Bowmar Records, Inc.

Singing Games. RCA Victor Basic Record Library for Elementary Schools. RCA Victor, E 87 or WE 87.

Singing Games. Albums 1 and 2. Bowmar Records, Inc.

Street Games and Songs, New York City. Ethnic Folkways, 7003.

Elementary Music Series Books

Most elementary school song books include a variety of folk games and dances suitable for use by the children. In the majority of the present-day series the directions are included in the children's books. Only a few of the many excellent games and dances can be listed here: "Four in a Boat," *Growing With Music*, Book 4; " 'Simmons," *This Is Music*, Book 4; "Turkey in the Straw," *Discovering Music Together*, Book 6; "Square Dance," *Making Music Your Own*, Book 4; "Totur," *Exploring Music*, Book 6; "Rain Dance Song," *The Magic of Music*, Book 3; "Caller's Song," *Studying Music* (*Music for Young Americans*, Book 6); "Red River Valley," *Basic Goals in Music*, Book 3.

PLAYING
RHYTHM INSTRUMENTS

The playing of rhythm instruments constitutes an important part of the basic rhythmic experience that children should have in the elementary school. Part II of this book is devoted to the subject "Classroom Instruments in the General Music Program," including rhythm instrument activities. See page 54 for the chapter that deals with "Traditional Rhythm Instruments in the Classroom" and page 63 for the chapter on "Folk and National Rhythm Percussion Instruments in the Classroom."

3

Getting Acquainted
with Rhythm Notation

Many boys and girls have difficulty learning to use rhythm notation because, although their minds may grasp the mathematical differences between notes of various lengths, they do not sense (or feel) the musical relationships. In order to use rhythm notation successfully, children must first of all have the ability to feel the rhythmic pulsations in music and to respond to them with movement. The development of this skill is discussed in Chapter 2. When children keep time to music they hear freely and easily, they are usually ready to begin the use of printed notation.

RECOGNIZING RHYTHM
PATTERNS BY EAR

It is impossible for students to use rhythm notation successfully and in a musical way until they can recognize by ear the differences between notes of varying lengths. This section presents activities for providing experiences in hearing, recognizing, and using the basic rhythm patterns. The class participates in all these activities *without* the use of notation; they follow the rhythms they *hear*. Many of the rhythm reading problems that boys and girls have as they sing and play stem directly from their inability to recognize by ear the rhythm patterns they are attempting to perform. The ear is of fundamental importance to the development of skills in reading music.

Suggested Activities

From a multitude of possible activities, only a few are included here. Older boys and girls enjoy and profit from experience with most of these activities, many of which can also be carried on successfully in classes of very young children.

1. *Distinguishing between long and short notes*
   a. The class listens while the teacher plays (on a drum or on the piano) a steadily moving series of notes such as quarter notes, at a moderate speed. This is followed by another series of notes twice as fast as the first, as eighth notes would be. The children recognize the difference between the long and the short notes.
   b. The teacher plays again and the children swing their arms lightly with each note heard, swinging slowly or fast according to the notes they hear.
   c. The children swing their arms and also walk, taking a step with every note heard. Each type of note, long or short, should be repeated enough times to allow the children to hear it and then to follow it in their movements. Some children need time to recognize a change in speed and to adjust their movements to it.
   d. The children move, using arms and feet as before, and this time also chanting for each note. (*Note:* There are many popular ways of chanting these notes. Some classes say "Walk" for each quarter note and "Run" for each eighth. A system that appears both in some current American music teaching materials and also in some very old books, and that has long been popular in European schools, uses "ta" for the quarter note and "ti" [tee] for the eighth notes. The use of words chanted to show recognition of notes of various lengths, whether "Walk, run-run" or "Slow, fast-fast" or "ta, ti-ti," or any similar device is suggested for the period when the ear is the only guide to the notes. After rhythm notation is introduced, the notes can be called "quarter" and "eighth"; before the notation is introduced however, word chants are helpful. They will aid the children in concentrating on what they are hearing and in responding with a specific movement suited to each note heard.)

e. Part of the group moves to the rhythm as before; some play rhythm instruments following each note; all chant.

2. *Hearing long and short notes that are sounded together*
   a. When most of the children can easily recognize the two types of notes and respond to them, divide the class into two groups, one to respond to quarter notes, the other to eighth notes. The teacher plays, alternating between a series of quarter notes and a series of eighth notes; each group responds in its turn.
   b. The two groups chant and move at the same time. This requires the development of the feeling for two eighth notes to one quarter note. The tempo must be rather slow so that all can easily *hear* the two-to-one relationship and can *move* and *chant* to show the difference clearly.

3. *Echo clapping*
   The teacher claps short rhythm groups such as those given below, and the class claps the same group, echoing it without a break in the rhythm. They can also chant and step as they echo what the teacher claps. (The notation given below is included here as an example for the *teacher*. It is not planned for use by the class in reading notation at this time.)

4. *Long and short notes in familiar songs*
   If a familiar song that uses only these quarter and eighth notes is available, learn it by rote. Sing it, stepping, swinging arms, or tapping softly to each note. Sometimes the children enjoy singing the rhythmic chant words ("walk, run"; "ta, ti"; etc.) to the melody in place of the words of the song while they move with the music. The tempo must be slow enough to allow the children to hear and move to the two types of notes.

ON THE BRIDGE OF AVIGNON

French Folk Song

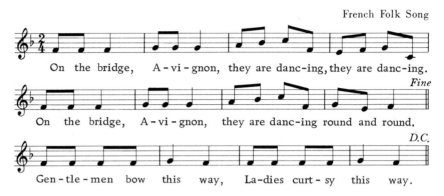

On the bridge,   A - vi - gnon,   they are danc-ing, they are danc-ing.

Fine

On   the   bridge,   A - vi - gnon,   they are danc-ing round and round.

D.C.

Gen - tle - men   bow   this   way,   La - dies   curt - sy   this   way.

5. *Other notes and rhythms*

Other rhythm elements and note groupings can be added later for recognition by ear and movement. These include the following notes and groups:

"skip - ty "; "ti - ty "

"slo - ow "; "ta - a "

"sto - o - op "; "ta - a - a "

The same types of activity suggested for quarter and eighth notes can be used in introducing each of these. It is wise to give time for extensive experience with each note or group alone and in combination with the others that were previously learned before progressing to others. Start each rhythmic experience of this kind by clearly establishing the tempo and beat, usually by sounding a series of quarter notes.

INTRODUCING RHYTHM NOTATION

When the basic notes and rhythm groups are familiar and easily recognized by ear, most classes are ready to learn to use rhythm notation. From a great many possible kinds of experiences that are helpful in developing understanding and skill in the use of the notes, only a few are included here.

Suggested Activities

1. *First use of ♩ and ♫*

a. The children sing a familiar song that uses the notes to be introduced first, in this case ♩ and ♫ . They swing their arms and tap
   softly with each note as they sing; at the same time the teacher
   puts a mark on the chalkboard for each note heard in the song.
   For example, the first phrase of the song "On the Bridge of Avi-
   gnon" would look like this:

   — — —   — — —   — — — — —   — — —

   The stems are added to produce the notes:

   ♫ ♩   ♫ ♩   ♫ ♫   ♫ ♫

   The children sing and tap again, this time using rhythmic chant
   words such as "run" and "walk" or "ti" and "ta," while watching
   the notes on the board as the teacher points to them. Individual
   children point out "walk" and "run" notes on the board. If the
   song is in their books, they open to it and sing, tapping each note.

b. The teacher can begin at once to call the notes by their correct
   names, "quarter" and "eighth," and can also show the various
   ways of writing them:

   ♩ ♩ ♫ ♫ ♪ ♪ ♪ ♪

c. Flash cards with easy groups of quarter and eighth notes (in $\frac{2}{4}$, $\frac{3}{4}$,
   or $\frac{4}{4}$ measure patterns) are displayed. The teacher plays one pattern on the woodblock while the class listens. The children
   identify what they have heard on the correct flash card and all
   tap (or step or chant) the pattern. Individual children demonstrate patterns for the class to recognize.

d. A felt board with an assortment of quarter and eighth notes is
   used. (Eighth notes grouped by two's, ♫ , are helpful for the first
   experience.) The teacher taps or claps a short group of quarter
   and eighth notes. The class listens and repeats the pattern, feeling

the long and short notes. Then they select the correct notes to put on the felt board.

e. A game: "Where Did I Stop?" The books are opened to a song that uses the familiar rhythm notation. The children watch the books, following the notes with fingers if necessary, while the teacher plays the rhythm of the song on the woodblock. She stops somewhere part way through the song, and the children point to the last note she played.

f. A round with the familiar rhythm notation is used:

SCOTLAND'S BURNING

Scot-land's burn-ing, Scot-land's burn-ing, Look out, look out, Fire! Fire! Fire! Fire! pour on wa-ter, pour on wa-ter.

The round is sung first in unison with rhythm accompaniment, clapping, tapping, stepping, or using rhythm instruments. Then the class is divided into two sections. Group 1 sings and claps, taps, steps, or uses rhythm instruments to produce its rhythm. Group 2 starts when Group 1 has finished the first two measures. The sound of each rhythm pattern should be light and clear enough to make it possible for the children to hear the two patterns as they are sounded together. The class can be divided into three or four sections when desired.

g. This kind of activity has great value in developing musicianship at every grade level and suitable songs are to be found in most current school song books. Here are some examples for introducing ♩ and ♫ : "Seven Steps," *Growing With Music*, Book 3; "Clap Your Hands," *Making Music Your Own*, Books 1 and 2; "Scotland's Burning," *Exploring Music*, Book 2; "Rain, Rain, Go Away," *Discovering Music Together*, Book 2; "Pony Trot," *This Is Music*, Book 2; "To Paree," *The Magic of Music*, Book 2; "Doodle, Doodle," *Discovering Music* (*Music for Young Americans*, Book 2); "God, Our Heav'nly Father," *Basic Goals in Music*, Book 2.

2. *Other notes and rhythms*

When ♩ and ♫ are familiar and can be used with some skill, other notes and rhythm patterns already familiar by ear can be introduced visually. The additional notes or groups are introduced gradually, usually only one new one at a time. Most school music series books at all levels contain suitable song material for this type of activity, since these rhythmic combinations are used continually. In addition to the following notes and groups, some books also include some materials for the introduction of the whole note.

a. *Songs for introducing* ♩. ♪ : "Grandma Said," *Growing With Music*, Book 3; "The Music Man," *This Is Music*, Book 2; "Yankee Doodle," *Exploring Music*, Book 2; "Turkey Beware," *Discovering Music* (*Music for Young Americans*, Book 2); "Tambur Andandori," *The Magic of Music*, Book 3; "Easter Fun," *Discovering Music Together*, Book 2; "Who Did?," *Basic Goals in Music*, Book 2.

b. *Songs for introducing* ♩ : "For a Leaf," *Growing With Music*, Book 3; "Puffer Billies," *This Is Music*, Book 4; "Kawakayima," *Making Music Your Own*, Book 2; "The Choo Choo," *Exploring Music*, Book 2; "Twinkle, Twinkle, Little Star," *The Magic of Music*, Book 2; "Are You Sleeping?" *Discovering Music Together*, Book 2; "Frère Jacques," *Discovering Music* (*Music for Young Americans*, Book 2); "Skip One Window," *Basic Goals in Music*, Book 2.

c. *Songs for introducing* ♩ : "Here We Go Skating," *The Magic of Music*, Book 2; "Oranges and Lemons," *Growing With Music*, Book 3; "Andulko, the Goose Girl," *This Is Music*, Book 4; "Ach Ja!," *Exploring Music*, Book 2; "Sky Music," *Discovering Music Together*, Book 2; "Down, Down, Down," *Discovering Music* (*Music for Young Americans*, Book 2); "Sommer, ade," *Making Music Your Own*, Book 2; "Fray Martín," *Basic Goals in Music*, Book 3.

3. Another rhythm grouping which appears in many of the songs the children sing is the triplet, with its division of a beat into *three* equal parts instead of the *two* parts that are already familiar. Many of the activities suggested above for other rhythm notation can be used to help make the triplet a familiar part of the music vocabulary of the boys and girls. Such sequences as the following can be tapped or played on rhythm instruments:

etc.

4. Songs that were originally learned by rote should sometimes be sung

with the books open. Often, such songs will be found to include complex rhythm patterns of notes and rests, which the children may not yet have learned. Much knowledge about music notation is absorbed through using music in this way, with no explanation or discussion of the new material. Such experience paves the way for the development of independent skill in reading music, and assures that many items in rhythm notation will be familiar in a general way before they are given special attention.

CHANTING

Many different forms of muscular coordination are needed in developing an understanding of musical rhythm and skill in responding to it. Muscular response using the whole body, and especially the arms, feet, head, and trunk, is basic to all rhythm learning. Activities using the speech organs are also important however, particularly for the development of skill in speaking and singing rhythmically.

Following are some examples of ways of using vocal chants. This type of activity is done entirely by rote and by ear at first, but later it proves very useful in developing understanding of rhythm notation.

Name Chants

Children have a special interest in names, particularly their own names. Names have rhythms, and experience in chanting them can develop skill in hearing and in producing various rhythm patterns of short and long or fast and slow sounds. Here are some activities for name chants:

1. The teacher starts by chanting the children's names, repeating each name several times rhythmically. The class imitates, chanting the names after her or with her.
2. A child chants his own name and the class repeats it after him.
3. The rhythm of a name is played on the woodblock. The children identify it and chant the name, tapping the rhythm.
4. Rhythm notation is added to the name chants in classes familiar with notes. Examples:

John,   John   ♩   ♩

Pe - ter,   P - ter

Ma - ri - lyn, Ma - ri - lyn

5. The children divide into groups, each group selecting instruments that seem to fit one of the chants, perhaps the small drum for "John, John"; rhythm sticks or woodblock for "Pe-ter, Pe-ter"; rattles or tambourine for "Ma-ri-lyn, Ma-ri-lyn." The groups chant and play one after the other, repeating each name perhaps four times. The recurring beat should be steady so that each chant of four words is equal in length to the others, although the sounds in "Pe-ter, Pe-ter" are obviously faster than those in "John, John."
6. Some classes are skillful enough to divide into groups and chant and play two or more names simultaneously. In such cases, it is important that the chanting and playing be steady and that the various names be begun together with careful precision. The rhythm instruments used should be played lightly but clearly.

Word Chants

Words and groups of words that are related and that have some special interest for the children can also be chanted. Carl Orff in his *Music for Children, I, Pentatonic,* uses the names of trees and flowers in this way. Similarly, the following can be chanted. The rhythm notation is added when appropriate, although this is not essential. It is important to tap the rhythm and play it, using percussion instruments, as well as to chant it.

Elm,   tree,

Tu - lip,   tu - lip

Sy - ca - more, sy - ca - more

Many other groups of words can be chanted in the same way. Children can create word chants, often also notating them: fall, fall, win-ter, winter; spring, spring, sum-mer, sum-mer; red, red, yel-low, yel-low; blue, blue, pur-ple, pur-ple.

Rhymes, Jingles,
and Traditional Chants

There are many familiar chants that give the children experience with the use of longer groups of words and notes than is provided by chanting names and single words. Some of these are commonly used by children in connection with play activities like skipping rope. Sometimes the same chant can be done to several different rhythms. Flash cards, felt board, and chalkboard can be used to reinforce knowledge of the rhythm notation of the chants in classes where this notation has been introduced. The jingles and rhymes can also be chanted and played as canons, as was suggested for the rounds under 1,f, page 20.

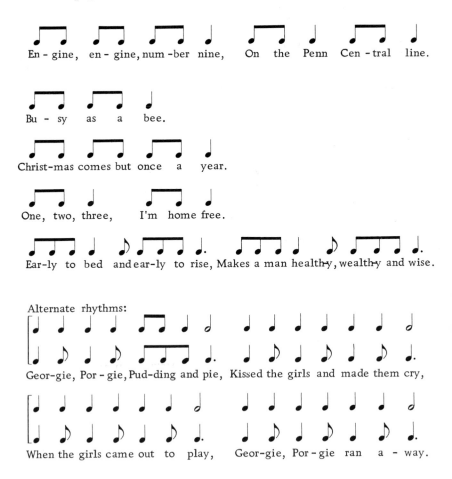

En - gine, en - gine, num -ber nine,   On   the   Penn   Cen -tral   line.

Bu - sy   as   a   bee.

Christ-mas comes but once   a   year.

One, two, three,   I'm   home free.

Ear-ly to bed and ear-ly to rise, Makes a man health-y, wealth-y and wise.

Alternate rhythms:

Geor-gie, Por - gie, Pud-ding and pie, Kissed the girls and made them cry,

When the girls came out to play,   Geor-gie, Por - gie ran   a - way.

Additional
Sources of Chants

Books

Garretson, Robert L., *Music in Childhood Education.* New York: Appleton-Century-Crofts, 1966.

Monsour, Sally, Marilyn Cohen, and Patricia Lindell, *Rhythm in Music and Dance.* Belmont, Calif: Wadsworth Publishing Company, Inc., 1966.

Nye, Robert E., and Bjornar Bergethon, *Basic Music: An Activities Approach to Functional Musicianship* (3rd ed.). Englewood Cliffs, N.J.: Prentice-Hall, Inc., 1968.

Nye, Robert E. and Vernice T. Nye, *Exploring Music With Children.* Belmont, Calif: Wadsworth Publishing Company, Inc., 1966.

————, *Music in the Elementary School* (3rd ed.). Englewood Cliffs, N.J.: Prentice-Hall, Inc., 1970.

Orff, Carl, and Gunild Keetman, *Music for Children, I, Pentatonic* (English adaptation by Doreen Hall and Arnold Walter). Mainz, Germany: B. Schott's Söhne, U.S.A. (Associated Music Publishers, New York).

Richards, Mary Helen, *Threshold to Music.* New York: Harper & Row, Publishers, 1964.

Records

Music for Children. Carl Orff, Gunild Keetman, and Walter Jelinek. Angel-Capitol Records B-3582.

Discovering Rhythm and Rhyme in Poetry. Louis Untermeyer, Julie Harris, and David Wayne. Caedmon Records TC 1156.

Elementary Music Series Books

Most of the current school series books include chants for use in connection with class activities. Here are some examples: "Making Up Music," *Growing With Music,* Books 2 and 3; "Creating Music," *Growing With Music,* Books 4, 5, and 6; "We Say and Play," *This Is Music,* Book 2; "I Like to Make Up Songs," *The Magic of Music,* Book 2; "Walking and Talking," "Promenade," "On the Move," *Meeting Music* (*Music for Young Americans,* Book 1); "Song of the Rain Chant," *Discovering Music Together,* Book 3; "The Porcupine," *Making Music Your Own,* Book 1; "Witches' Cauldron," *Basic Goals in Music,* Book 3.

ACCENT AND METER:
MEASURE SIGNATURE

When children pay attention to the various types of notes that appear in printed form in their books, they will also begin to be interested in other noticeable features related to rhythm notation, such as measure signature and measure bars. As is the case with most phases of rhythm learning, the understanding of these new elements is developed first through hearing and making movement response to the rhythm of music. Knowledge about the printed symbols follows this recognition by ear and movement. Here are some suggested activities for use in developing this understanding of the measure divisions in music. $\frac{2}{4}$, $\frac{3}{4}$, and $\frac{4}{4}$ meters are included here. Other meters are discussed in later sections of this chapter.

1. The children tap or clap their hands or play rhythm instruments in time to the accents they hear in music. Each time they respond to an accent they also chant, "1." Phonograph records or the piano can be used to produce the music, or the class can be divided into two sections, one of which sings while the other taps and chants the "1." The music should be steady and well-accented. (For example, the following will provide a variety of usable music: selected marches and waltzes from *The Rhythm Program, Vols. I and II, RCA Victor Basic Record Library for Elementary Schools*, RCA Victor, E-71-72 or WE 71-72; *America's Favorite Marches*, RCA Victor LPM 1175.)

2. The children listen to music with a steady, clearly defined sequence of accented and unaccented beats. They tap and chant the "1" as usual, and then try to discover the number of unaccented beats between the "one's." Making the "1" a stronger accent than the other beats, they tap and count the meter, "1-2-3, 1-2-3" or "1-2, 1-2" or "1-2-3-4, 1-2-3-4." Whether recorded music, piano music, or songs are used, the music should be at a speed suitable for hearing and responding to the recurring accented and unaccented beats. When songs are used, some of the children sing while the others find and count the beats.

3. The children walk to the music, marking the accented and unaccented beats with contrasting heavy and light steps. Some children find it easier to do this if they clap or tap the accented and unaccented beats with their hands while they walk.

4. Here is a song that can be used with the activities suggested above.

FOUR IN A BOAT

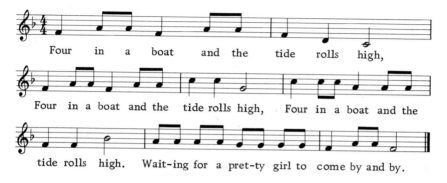

Four   in   a   boat   and   the   tide   rolls   high,

Four   in   a   boat   and   the   tide rolls   high,   Four   in   a   boat   and   the

tide rolls   high.   Wait-ing for   a   pret-ty   girl to   come by and by.

From *Growing With Music*, Book 4, p. 41. © 1966 by Prentice-Hall, Inc.

The children look at the notation of the song, which they have previously learned by rote. It may be on the board or in the books. One group sings the song while the others chant the "1" and tap on the accent. Attention is called to the bar line, which comes before each "1" except at the very beginning of the song. Most classes understand a definition such as: "These lines measure off the notes into equal groups between the accents or '1's.' They are called measure bars." They notice the measure signature, $\frac{4}{4}$. "The lower number '4' refers to a quarter note. The upper number '4' tells us that in this song it takes four of these quarter notes, or other notes equal to them, to fill a measure." (*Note:* In this song and, in fact, frequently in the music the children use, the upper number in the time signature indicates also the number of *beats* in a measure, but this is not always true. It is important that the children learn from the first that the upper number really simply shows how many notes of the value of the lower number [or their equivalent] are needed to *fill* a measure in the music. The kind of note that receives one beat depends on the speed or tempo of the music.) At this time, or soon after, the children will probably discover the use of C as a substitute for $\frac{4}{4}$ in some of their music.

5. The same types of activity can be carried on with familiar songs with the signature $\frac{3}{4}$ if they are sung at a tempo in which the quarter note receives a beat. (Many favorite songs in $\frac{3}{4}$ are sung so fast that it is really ♩. that receives a beat—there is only *one* beat in a measure, even though it requires three quarter notes to *fill* a mea-

sure.) The $\frac{2}{4}$ measure is also easily introduced in the same way with the use of a familiar song. Frequent brief periods of attention to the elements of rhythm notation will soon develop both understanding and skill in the use of the notes. In choosing songs for these first lessons about measure divisions, it is suggested that the music chosen begin with a full measure and not with an "upbeat," and that the note values included be familiar. The lesson is more assured of success if the children can concentrate on learning just one new thing at a time and not a series of complex unfamiliar elements. Some examples of songs useful for these lessons are: "Are You Sleeping?" *Growing With Music*, Book 3; "Circle Around," *Exploring Music*, Book 2; Units 2, 3, and 5, *Discovering Music* (*Music for Young Americans*, Book 2); "French Cradle Song" and "The Beat of Music," "Meter," and "Tempo," *The Magic of Music*, Book 3; "Sur le Pont" and "Navajo Happy Song," *This Is Music*, Book 3; "Sky Music," *Discovering Music Together*, Book 2; "Bounce High, Bounce Low," *Making Music Your Own*, Book 2; "Four in the Boat," *Basic Goals in Music*, Book 2.

6. There are many kinds of games that can provide challenge and competition in the recognition and use of the various kinds of measures. Flash cards can be used with familiar measure signatures ($\frac{2}{4}$, $\frac{3}{4}$, $\frac{4}{4}$), each followed by a few measures of notes, some correctly filled and some wrong. The children identify and clap out the correct measures; they decide on the necessary changes to correct the wrong measures. Older boys and girls who write with ease can compete to see who can fill the greatest number of measures using familiar note values and measure signatures.

7. Children enjoy learning to conduct some of the songs they sing in which the familiar meters are used, emphasizing the accented "1" downbeat in contrast to the unaccented beats. See: *The Magic of Music*, Book 4, pp. 21, 24, 25, 29; *Making Music Your Own*, Book 4, pp. 31, 40, 78; *Exploring Music* (*Music for Young Americans*, Book 3), "Conducting Music" (*Learning About Music*, Unit Two, 42ff); *Studying Music* (*Music for Young Americans*, Book 6), "You Can Be a Conductor" (*Learning About Music*, Unit Seven, 138ff); *This Is Music*, Book 7, p. 32.

8. As the children's experience increases, they can add new measure signatures to those already familiar. In addition to those already mentioned, the meters most commonly found in the song materials in elementary school music books are $\frac{2}{2}$ (or the symbol $\mathbb{C}$) and $\frac{3}{2}$. An introduction through a familiar song as was suggested above for other meters can well be used for helping children make the acquaintance of these new measure signatures.

ANACRUSIS
OR UPBEAT

Some of the songs in the children's books begin with an incomplete measure or anacrusis, also called by various other names such as "pickup" and "upbeat." Understanding of this can be developed through the use of a familiar song such as the following.

WE WISH YOU A MERRY CHRISTMAS

Traditional English Song

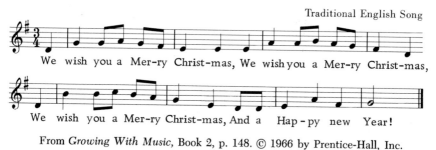

We wish you a Mer-ry Christ-mas, We wish you a Mer-ry Christ-mas,

We wish you a Mer-ry Christ-mas, And a   Hap - py   new   Year!

From *Growing With Music*, Book 2, p. 148. © 1966 by Prentice-Hall, Inc.

1. The books are closed and only the words to the song are on the board in four lines, as below.

    We *wish* you a mer-ry *Christ*-mas,
    We *wish* you a mer-ry *Christ*-mas,
    We *wish* you a mer-ry *Christ*-mas,
    And a *hap*-py New *Year.*

    The children chant the words to feel the accent or "1" and the unaccented beats. As they chant, the teacher underlines the words or syllables that are accented. The children notice that there is a word before the accent in each of the first three lines, and there are two words before the accent at the beginning of the last line.
2. Open the books to the song or look at the music elsewhere on the board. Notice the single quarter note that comes before the first full measure in each of the first three staves, and the two eighth notes at the beginning of the last one. Experiment by chanting the words as they would be if the upbeat were on an accented beat. Notice that the musical accents help to emphasize important words to make each phrase meaningful.
3. Boys and girls very gradually develop understanding of the fact that these unaccented beginning notes provide the beats to fill the incomplete measures in the song. Those who play piano or band or orches-

tra instruments will find that much instrumental music, where no words are involved, also begins with one or more unaccented first notes.

Sources:
Music for Teaching
the Anacrusis or Upbeat

Songs chosen for these first lessons should have familiar measure signatures and note values: "Good Night to You All," *Growing With Music,* Book 2. "Traffic Lights," *Discovering Music (Music for Young Americans,* Book 2); "My Father," *Discovering Music Together,* Book 2; "Sandy McNab," *Exploring Music,* Book 3; "For Health and Strength," *Making Music Your Own,* Book 3; "Little Bird on My Window," *The Magic of Music,* Book 2; "The Day is Now Over," *This Is Music,* Book 2; "Bluebells of Scotland," *Basic Goals in Music,* Book 2.

RESTS

Rests are best learned as they appear in the songs the children sing. Here are some suggestions for introducing them.

1. The first rest to be learned is usually the quarter rest. In most current music books, the quarter rest is 𝄽, but in some music the older form 𝄾, is used. The quarter rest is easily understood if the quarter note is already known. A familiar song such as this one, previously learned by rote, can be used.

LEFT, RIGHT, LEFT, RIGHT

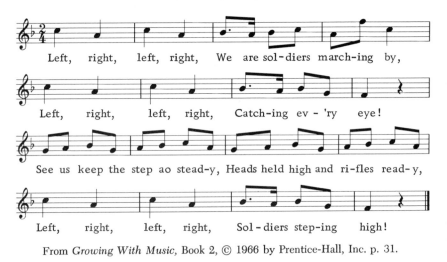

Left,   right,   left,   right,   We are sol-diers march-ing by,

Left,   right,   left,   right,   Catch-ing ev - 'ry   eye!

See us keep the step ao stead-y, Heads held high and ri-fles read-y,

Left,   right,   left,   right,   Sol - diers step-ing   high!

From *Growing With Music,* Book 2, © 1966 by Prentice-Hall, Inc. p. 31.

The rest is presented to the children simply as a sign for silence—for a period of silence as long as the equivalent note (in this case a one-beat quarter note) lasts. Chant the rhythm notation, part of the class chanting and the others singing. The only new point is that the rest is observed and its value recognized. It is chanted silently, or in a whisper.

2. Using the same idea, the children can also use rhythmic movement with the song, stepping, clapping, tapping, or playing rhythm instruments. They make the same steady rhythmic movement for the rest as for the notes, but the response to the rest is a silent one, or at least it is very quiet.

3. Many other different activities can be used to develop skill in singing and playing music in which the quarter rest appears. Simply-constructed measures or groups of measures are soon easily recognized when heard or seen, and they can be chanted or played or tapped or stepped. This can be done as a game: "Which group of notes is he tapping?"

A felt board with a variety of notes and rests available will make it possible for the children to picture groups of notes and rests they hear chanted or tapped. They can also experiment with creating original measures using familiar meter signatures.

4. Other rests are introduced as they are needed in developing understanding of the notation of the music being used. They should always be related to their equivalent notes.

Additional examples of songs for use in studying rests: "Winter Lullaby," *Growing With Music,* Book 3; "Pease Porridge Hot," *Making Music Your Own,* Book 3; "The Postman," *Exploring Music (Music for Young Americans,* Book 3); "Lights," *The Magic of Music,* Book 2; "Winter Is Over," *Exploring Music,* Book 2; "The Merry-Go-Round," *Discovering Music Together,* Book 2; "If You're Happy," *This Is Music,* Book 2; "Whistle, Daughter," *Basic Goals in Music,* Book 2.

THE TIE

Children who have had some experience with basic rhythmic activity and with the use of rhythm notation will begin to be curious about the *tie* as a special symbol. As with most such symbols, little explanation is needed; understanding comes gradually by linking the known with the new. For the introduction, it is suggested that a song previously learned by rote be used, preferably one that includes only notes whose rhythm values are already very familiar. It is wise also to start with a song in which the tie links two notes, each of which is one or more full beats in length, rather than notes that are less than one beat in length.

SKATER'S WALTZ

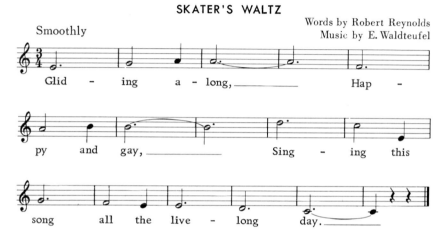

From *Growing With Music*, Book 3, p. 97. © 1966 by Prentice-Hall, Inc.

1. Review the song, singing it by rote at a moderately slow speed. Keep time by clapping or tapping softly on the accent or "1." Have one group sing and the other group count "1-2-3, 1-2-3" throughout. Look closely at the song in the book, singing the words and tapping under each note. Notice that while there are two 3-beat notes on "long" and "gay," the voice sings just one word—really, just one note. Identify the curved line as a "tie," which literally ties two notes together, making just one note of them, a note equal in length to the two notes. Notice the tie for "day" and discover the length.
2. The visual-minded child often grasps this idea through the use of two pieces of string knotted together. The tie in music ties together the two notes, making one note of them just as the knot in the string ties together the two pieces, making one piece of string. Sometimes the two are equal in length; sometimes one is longer than the other.
3. It may be wise at this time to call attention to the difference in looks and in function between the *tie*, which connects two notes on the same line or space, and the *slur*, which connects notes on different lines or spaces.

Additional examples of songs for introducing the tie: "Mañana," *Making Music Your Own,* Book 4; "Come Rowing with Me," *Discovering Music Together,* Book 2; "Lullaby," *This Is Music,* Book 3; "Come Boating with Me," *Exploring Music,* Book 3; "The Call of the Ocean," *The Magic of Music,* Book 3; "The Skaters' Waltz," *Exploring Music (Music for Young Americans,* Book 3); "Du, Du, Liegst Mir Im Herzen," *Basic Goals in Music,* Book 3.

SIX-EIGHT MEASURE ($\frac{6}{8}$)
AND OTHER
RELATED METERS

The six-eight measure signature sometimes causes problems for young learners because of the fact that there are really two different kinds of music that use this meter. There is the slow-moving music in which there are six beats in a measure, with an eighth note as the beat note. The fast-moving six-eight measure is far more common, however; many of the songs children sing and much of the rhythmic music they hear and move to will be found to be in fast six eight, with only two clearly defined beats in a measure. This latter type is the one boys and girls will meet most often, and therefore it is the one that is considered here. Children find this to be an easy rhythm to learn if it is presented clearly and simply.

For introducing this type of six-eight measure, choose a song that is normally sung at a fast-moving tempo. A simply constructed song that uses beat-units of ♩. , ♫♩ ♩ ♪ is easiest to use for the first lessons. The later use of songs in which a variety of rhythm combinations of notes and rests are found will not cause difficulty if the concept of two beat-units in a measure has been established. Here is a song that can provide an easy introduction to this rhythm.

LITTLE TOM TINKER

1. The class sings the familiar song (without the music) with a quick, swinging rhythm, keeping time by clapping or tapping. Divide into two sections; one sings and the other finds the "1," and then counts and taps the beats. They discover that they are counting "1-2, 1-2."

2. Open the books to the song or use the notes from a chart or the chalkboard. The two groups sing the song and count again, tapping in the books, moving the hand to tap under the note on which each beat begins. The teacher or a student can do this at the chart or board if books are not used. Find the measures that have only two notes; notice that these are dotted quarters.

3. Look at the measure signature: ⁶⁄₈. Some elementary-school songbooks picture this very clearly thus: ⁶⁄₈ (♩.). If this is not in the books, the teacher can put it on the board. Children have no difficulty in understanding this measure signature if they have already learned (as was suggested on page 27) that in a measure signature, the upper number shows how many notes of the value of the lower number are needed to fill a measure; that the number of beats depends on the speed or tempo of the music.

4. Discover the notes or groups of notes that are used to fill measures in this song:

Tap or clap each of these groups several times; play them, using rhythm instruments; go from one line to another as the teacher points to them. When they are familiar and easily used, divide into four groups and play or tap all these notes together. Use a speed that helps the children to hear the three fast notes clearly in relation to the other groups. Compare the sound and the notation of a beat divided into equal parts in ²⁄₄ measure and in fast ⁶⁄₈ measure:

Tap and play many such groups, going from one to the other until they are very familiar.

5. The children can also chant to these notes, using neutral syllables like "la" or "ta" (♩), "ti-ti-ti" (♫♪), or "ta-ti, ta-ti" (♩ ♪ ♩ ♪). Some classes use "walk" for the dotted quarter note, "run" for the eighth note, "skip-ty" for the quarter-eighth group, and "slo-ow" for the dotted half.

6. The children can use these beat-groups to make measures in various ways; then play, tap or chant their measures.

7. As other songs in fast six-eight measure are learned, new beat-units will be discovered and learned: ♩. ♫ , ♫ ♪ ♩ , etc. Here are some examples from current elementary-school music books of simply-constructed songs suitable for these introductory lessons: "Lullaby of the Wind," *Growing With Music*, Book 4; "I'se the B'y," *Making Music Your Own*, Book 4; "Row Your Boat," *Exploring Music* (*Music for Young Americans*, Book 3); "Row, Row, Row Your Boat," *The Magic of Music*, Book 3; "The Thread Follows the Needle," *Discovering Music Together*, Book 3; "Blow the Wind Southerly," *Exploring Music*, Book 4; "Rig-a-Jig-Jig," *This Is Music*, Book 4; "Oliver Cromwell," *Basic Goals in Music*, Book 4.

8. Other experiences of this kind can include specific attention to $\frac{3}{8}$ meter, which sometimes is counted in 3's, each separate eighth note receiving a beat, and at other times actually has just one beat to a measure, ♩. . The speed of the music is the deciding factor. Similarly $\frac{9}{8}$ and $\frac{12}{8}$ measure signatures are usually three beats ($\frac{9}{8}$) or four beats ($\frac{12}{8}$) to a measure.

Another familiar meter, $\frac{6}{4}$, is organized like $\frac{6}{8}$, but with different notes making up the various beat combinations. Children are much interested to discover that such groups as the following from these two meters can sound exactly alike, depending again on the tempo of the music.

Any of these meters will be challenging to children and can be learned without great difficulty if it appears in a clearly organized form in music the children want to sing or play. Like all concepts in music theory, these various measure signatures are important only when they are needed in order to produce music.

DOTTED QUARTER
AND EIGHTH ♩. ♪

In $\frac{6}{8}$ meter, the dotted quarter note is frequently the beat unit, as described above. In music in which the quarter note is the beat unit in $\frac{2}{4}$, $\frac{3}{4}$, or $\frac{4}{4}$ meter, special attention needs to be given to the rhythm pattern ♩. ♪ so that children can learn to use it when it occurs in music they sing and play. Children sing rote songs in which this pattern is used long before they learn to read it independently. Most of the school music series books include actual study of ♩. ♪ only in the later elementary grades.

Understanding of the less complex rhythm patterns, such as those included in the early sections of this chapter, should be developed before the following activities are introduced. A familiar rote song can be used to introduce the dotted quarter-eighth note group, and it is important to make sure that the rhythm pattern is correctly and precisely sung. A familiar song, such as "America the Beautiful," can be used in teaching this rhythm.

1. Sing the song without the books, tapping lightly to the rhythm of the words. The class will quickly notice the uneven movement of some sections of the song.
2. Open the books to the song. Sing and tap again, identifying the notes and words associated with the uneven pattern.
3. Divide the class into two sections. Everyone sings the song again, one section tapping the steady quarter note beats, and the other the rhythm pattern of the words.
4. Put two lines of notes on the board for the two sections of the class to tap, play on rhythm instruments, or chant. Sometimes play each line separately, alternating; sometimes play them together. Example:

♩ ♩ ♩ ♩ | ♩. ♩ ♩ |

♩. ♪♩ ♩ | ♩. ♪♩ |

5. The dot is usually defined as adding to a note half of its original value. However, most children comprehend and develop skill with this rhythm pattern better through a variety of activities that use both movement and visual experience, rather than through memorizing a definition. Here is a set of groupings that sometimes helps boys and girls to understand the numerical values of the notes by seeing them in several different written forms.

6. When clapping, tapping, or playing a rhythm instrument in response to the notes in a measure in which this rhythm pattern occurs, children usually need to give a silent swing to make the beat that falls on the dot, thus:

tap   swing tap   tap   tap

Without this swing to indicate a feeling for the duration of this beat, boys and girls often fail to give the dotted quarter note its full value.

Additional examples of songs for introducing ♩. ♪ : "America," *Growing With Music,* Book 4; "La Tarara," *Making Music Your Own,* Book 4; "Take Your Things and Go," *Understanding Music (Music for Young Americans,* Book 4); "We Sing of Golden Mornings," *Exploring Music,* Book 4; "The Birch Tree," *This Is Music,* Book 4; "All Through the Night," *The Magic of Music,* Book 3; "Goodbye, Old Paint," *Discovering Music Together,* Book 4; "Doon the Moor," *Basic Goals in Music,* Book 4.

GROUPS OF
SIXTEENTH NOTES
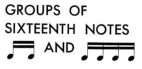

The use of groups of notes that divide a beat into small sections is not difficult for most classes to understand. Children sing many songs that include ♫♫ and ♫ before they first study the notation for these patterns. Previous to the experiences suggested below, the boys and girls should be able to respond to a steady rhythmic beat, both by moving to the music and by chanting simple rhythms. Usually, they will also be familiar with basic rhythm notation, probably including the notes, rests, and meters previously discussed.

1. Select a familiar song that includes ♫♫ and ♫ .

KOOKABURRA

Australian Round

Koo-ka-bur-ra sits on an old gum tree,— Mer-ry, mer-ry king of the bush is he,—— Laugh, koo-ka-bur-ra, Laugh, koo-ka-bur-ra, Gay your life must be.

From *Growing With Music*, Book 4, p. 155. © 1966 by Prentice-Hall, Inc.

The class sings the song at a moderate tempo, tapping the beats lightly with fingers, "1-2, 1-2," etc.

2. Sing the song again, this time tapping fingertips to the rhythm pattern of the words. Look at the words and the rhythm notation of the parts of the song that include sixteenth notes:

"Koo-ka-bur-ra"  ; "sits on an"

3. Sing the song again using a repeated neutral syllable for each note, perhaps, "Ta-ta-ta-ta-," etc. Play the notes lightly on a rhythm instrument such as the wood block.

4. Put various combinations of familiar groups of notes, including the sixteenth notes on the board:

Chant these rhythm patterns on a neutral syllable and tap fingers lightly. Repeat each line several times.

5. Select rhythm instruments suitable for light, quick movements and play rhythm patterns like the preceding ones, all instruments in unison. Then play again, but this time alternate, with a different instrument for each pattern. Play (and chant) as a canon, one instrument starting with the first pattern and continuing through all the pat-

terns. A second instrument begins when the first starts the second line, and the others follow in turn until all are playing (and chanting) together.

6. Make simple rhythm instrument accompaniments for songs in which these sixteenth-note patterns occur. For example, for "Kookaburra," the accompaniment might be:

It will often be easier for the children to play these patterns clearly and lightly if both hands are used on an instrument, alternating thus:

It is important to use a tempo moderate enough to allow children to play these patterns easily, but not so slow as to ruin the rhythmic swing of the music.

Additional materials suggested for introducing groups of sixteenth notes: "Hush-a-by," *Growing With Music,* Book 3; "Kookaburra," *Making Music Your Own,* Book 3; "My Pretty Little Miss," *This Is Music,* Book 2; "Tirra Lirra Loo," *Understanding Music* (*Music for Young Americans,* Book 4); "Pick a Pumpkin," *The Magic of Music,* Book 2; "Old Brass Wagon," *Discovering Music Together,* Book 4; "The Happy Plowman," *Exploring Music,* Book 4; "Michael Finnigan," *Basic Goals in Music,* Book 4.

SYNCOPATION

Another type of rhythm organization which children need to experience is syncopation. They are familiar with it and respond to it naturally when they use much of the so-called popular music and they are often surprised and interested to discover that the same type of rhythm appears frequently in other music, especially in some of the folksongs they sing. They have learned to swing, tap, clap, and use rhythm instruments to keep time to music, feeling the accent on "1" and counting the related unaccented beats. It is fascinating to find that the catchy syncopated rhythms are the result of shifting the accent and putting it in an unexpected place.

Syncopation has been important in our popular music from the days of ragtime, and later jazz, and on to the present popular songs. It also appears in much of the standard composed music. This is an area of musical experience that is very important to today's boys and girls. Many of the current elementary-school music books help them get acquainted with syncopation as a means of changing the rhythm pattern in music, giving it a special flavor that is usually very attractive to children.

Many songs have syncopated rhythms that are highly complex in structure, and children in a general classroom will usually profit most from learning such songs by rote, perhaps from a record. A familiar song in which there are syncopated rhythms that are *not* complex is best for introducing children to the idea of syncopation. A favorite song of this type is "The Erie Canal."[1] Just the first two measures of this song give the flavor of the syncopated rhythm.

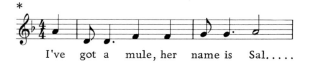

I've got a   mule, her   name is   Sal.....

From *Growing With Music*, Book 5, p. 76. © 1966 by Prentice-Hall, Inc.

Have the children clap or tap the rhythm of these words. Now have them sing the same words and tune using an even rhythm, and notice the change.

I've got a mule her   name is Sal......

Divide the class into two groups, one of which taps the even, steady rhythm, while the other taps the syncopated rhythm. Use rhythm instruments, having some tap the steady beats (perhaps with the tom-tom or the

[1] The entire song can be found in *Growing With Music*, Book 5, p. 76.

wood block) while others play the syncopated rhythm (perhaps with tambourine or rattles).

Look for examples of syncopation in other songs. Some famous examples include: "Rock Island Line," *Growing With Music*, Book 5; "John Henry," *Making Music Your Own*, Book 5; "Canoe Song," *Discovering Music Together*," Book 5; "Come to the Land," *Exploring Music*, Book 5; "Ground Hog," *This Is Music*, Book 5; "Take Your Partner's Hand," *The Magic of Music*, Book 5; "South of the Border," *Understanding Music* (*Music for Young Americans*, Book 4); "Canoe Song," *Basic Goals in Music*, Book 4.

MUSIC WITH
CHANGING METERS

A constantly increasing amount of the music that boys and girls will be singing and playing does not use the same meter throughout a song or instrumental composition. The meter may change, and sometimes does so frequently. Some of this music has been written by contemporary composers; some comes from the distant past; some is found in certain types of folk music.

Learning to recognize music in which the meter changes and to enjoy performing it is not difficult for children who have had past experience with basic meters and rhythm notation as previously suggested. Experience in responding to rhythm and meter through movement is an important preparation for the intelligent grasp of music in which the meter changes. In a song, this type of rhythm organization is often a result of the fact that the music follows the changing accents in the words. Songs, therefore, provide an easy introduction to the reading of notation where the meter changes.

Unless the music gives specific instructions that the beat unit is to be changed when the measure signature changes, the beat remains constant. If the children are accustomed to tapping or clapping the beats, they will be intrigued and interested in the shifting accents that are a feature of music in which the meter changes. Here are some suggestions for introduction of this type of music:

1. Start with a familiar song that has been learned by rote. For the first presentation, this will preferably be a song in which the kind of note that receives a beat remains the same, even when the meter changes.

MY WAGON

Netherlands Folk Song
Translation by Beth Landis

1. O my wag - on is well - lad - en, full of scold - ing
2. O my wag - on is well - lad - en, full of schem - ing
3. O my wag - on is well - lad - en, full of fair young

wo - men, O they quar - rel and they chat - ter, peace I'm
grand-dads, O they're plot - ting and they're plant-ing, how I
la - dies, O they sing - ing and they're chat- ting, and their

nev - er giv - en; Nev - er a - gain I'll take, for
tire of those lads; Nev - er a - gain I'll take, for
smiles do me please; Now once a - gain I'll take, for

my part, Chat - ter -ing wo-men in my horse - cart!
my part, Schem-ing old grand-dads in my horse - cart!
my part, Fair - est young la-dies in my horse - cart!

Hup, horse, get up!
Hup, horse, get up!
Hup, horse, get up!

From *Exploring Music, 5.* Eunice Boardman and Beth Landis. Holt, Rinehart and Winston, Inc., publishers. © 1966.

Open the books to the song. Let the children discover the meter changes.

2. Divide the class into two groups. One group sings the song while the second group taps and counts, "3-1-2-3, 1-2-3," accenting the "1" slightly. Where the meter changes, the speed of the quarter note beat remains the same, but the counting changes to "1-2" and then "1-2-3-4," etc.

3. When new songs in which the meter changes are learned using nota- tion, be sure that the changes are noticed in advance of reading the notes. Establish the meter and speed of the first section of the music,

tapping and counting. Then have one group chant the long and short notes in the song, perhaps using the words, while the other group taps and counts the meter throughout. This will show the relationship of the word accents to the meter changes.

4. As new songs with changing meters are learned, some may be found in which the kind of note receiving a beat changes when the meter changes. (For example, sometimes the beat unit changes from $\quad$ in $\frac{2}{4}$ to $\quad$ in $\frac{6}{8}$; or from $\quad$ in $\frac{2}{2}$ to $\quad$ in $\frac{2}{4}$.) Usually in such cases there is a tempo marking that shows that the speed of the beat remains the same, although the kind of note receiving a beat changes. Sometimes, however, the beat becomes faster or slower. This situation provides a good opportunity to teach boys and girls to learn to use tempo markings, if they have not already learned this.

Additional sources of songs with changing meters: "Coffee Grows on White Oak Trees," *Growing With Music,* Book 4; "Shenandoah," *Making Music (Music for Young Americans,* Book 5); "A Little Ship," *Making Music Your Own,* Book 4; "Come, Come Ye Saints," *This Is Music,* Book 5; "Shenandoah," *Discovering Music Together,* Book 4; "In the Fireplace," *The Magic of Music,* Book 3; "Spring," *Basic Goals in Music,* Book 6.

INTRODUCING MUSIC
WITH UNUSUAL METERS
($\frac{5}{4}$, $\frac{7}{8}$, etc.)

Sometimes the children find among their songs or instrumental music some compositions in which there are different meters from those found in most of the music with which they are familiar. These unusual meters are often found in contemporary composed music and also in the folk music of certain countries. There are songs using such meters in most of the elementary-school music books and children can learn to understand the relationship of the music to the words, and the reason for the unevenly organized measures. If the class understands and can use the basic, familiar types of meters, such as $\frac{4}{4}$, $\frac{3}{4}$, and $\frac{6}{8}$, and the notes and rests which appear in them, they will have no difficulty with the unusual groupings. They will, in fact, usually be greatly interested in them. Children's own musical creations frequently use meters that are not traditional, but are freely organized.

1. Preparation for introduction to these unusual meters can be made effectively through the use of a drum on which the teacher plays

various measure groupings some of which are familiar and some unusual. The children listen and identify the meters by finding the accented "1" and counting the beats. Examples of some possible drum rhythms for this type of activity:

Each measure grouping should be repeated several times until the majority of the children sense it and can tap and count it. Put the notes for such measures as the above on the board and have the children listen to them and recognize them as they are heard.

2. Open the books to a familiar song that has an unusual meter. Here is an example:

LEGEND

From *Studying Music* (*Music for Young Americans*, Book 6), Richard C. Berg *et al.* American Book Co., publishers. © 1963 and 1959.

Notice the measure signature. Divide the class into two groups. One group sings the song, while the others tap and count the   measure, accenting the "1." There are frequently also secondary accents in meters such as $\frac{5}{4}$ or $\frac{7}{4}$. These accents can group the notes in several different ways. In a song it is usually the words that govern the grouping. In some folk dances the shifting accents are necessary to synchronize the music and the steps. Put the following measure divisions on the board. One group of children sings "Legend" and the other group watches the notes as they listen to the song. They easily discover that the accents in the first group of notes are used in this song.

♩ ♩ ♩ ♩ ♩ or ♩ ♩ ♩ ♩ ♩
  >   >   >   >

3. Find and use the other songs and examples of instrumental music in meter.

4. When other unusual meter signatures appear in the music being sung or played, study them using the notation, tapping or clapping and sometimes also chanting to feel the word rhythms.

5. Listen for and recognize examples of these meters in instrumental music that is heard in listening lessons. Examples: "Promenade" from *Pictures at an Exhibition,* Mussorgsky (see *The Magic of Music,* Book 4, page 114 and *Exploring Music,* Book 4, page 114); Second Movement, *Sixth Symphony,* Tschaikowsky; and selections from *Mikrokosmos,* Bartók.

Additional music suggested for singing and playing in the classroom: "Gerakina," *Making Music Your Own,* Book 6; "The Queen Bee," *Discovering Music Together,* Book 6; "How Far to Bethlehem?," *Exploring Music,* Book 5; No. 5 in "Ostinato Pieces," *Minor-Bordun, Vol. IV, Music for Children (Orff-Schulwerk.* See p. 127).

PART II

USING CLASSROOM INSTRUMENTS IN THE GENERAL MUSIC PROGRAM

4

Introduction

CLASSROOM INSTRUMENTS

The term *classroom instruments* is a descriptive term applied to musical instruments that can be played by many or all of the students in a general classroom as part of the usual music activities of the group. Frequently, these are instruments that were made specifically for playing in the general music class. Sometimes standard musical instruments (wind, percussion, string, keyboard) are employed as classroom instruments through the use of such relatively uncomplicated playing activities as can be participated in by boys and girls who may not have had special music instruction outside the schoolroom. Included in this group are instruments of the band and the orchestra and other instruments of special types, such as the guitar and the recorder. In addition a wide variety of folk and national instruments from many parts of the world can be used in the musical activities of the classroom.

VALUES OF CLASSROOM INSTRUMENT ACTIVITY

Experience in playing classroom instruments can have many valuable results in the general music class.

1. Opportunity is supplied for many activities that are of immediate interest to boys and girls, that challenge thought and action, and that help them discover the fact that participation in the music class can be a pleasurable experience.
2. An excellent means is provided for developing the basic music skills needed by children if they are to use and enjoy music as an area of importance in everyday life. Some of these skills are:

   a. Keeping time to music.
   b. Using the ears in the recognition and playing of rhythm and melody patterns heard in music and in discovering the underlying harmonic organization.
   c. Using basic music notation in singing and in playing.
   d. Learning to hear, to play, and to sing music in more than one part.
   e. Developing taste and discrimination in creating simple rhythms, melodies, and song accompaniments.

3. Classroom instrument activity can furnish an excellent means of taking care of individual differences. Some of these instruments are valuable because they provide wide and varied opportunities for gifted children to learn more about music and to participate in musical activities that challenge their skill and imagination. On the other hand, some of these instruments are particularly useful in the classroom because of the ease with which they can be successfully played by children with poorly developed musical skills and those with physical, mental, and emotional difficulties.
4. Through playing these instruments, children sometimes discover special interests and abilities that may lead them to seek further satisfaction through the study of standard performing instruments.
5. The experience of hearing and playing instruments that are folk and national in character can aid in developing an understanding of the indigenous music of people in many parts of the world and incidentally can also help bring about a respect for the cultures of the ethnic groups represented.
6. Classroom instrumental experiences can provide a valuable opportunity for creative activity in the general classroom.

TYPES OF
CLASSROOM INSTRUMENTS

1. *Rhythm instruments.* These are instruments used to emphasize the basic rhythm, to enhance the rhythmic pattern of the music, and to accompany the songs and dances of ethnic groups. Included are:

a. *Traditional school rhythm instruments* such as are found in most elementary schools.

b. *Folk and national rhythm instruments,* which can be used by boys and girls to enrich their learning of the folk music of various lands and peoples. Included are instruments such as those of Latin America, Africa, the Orient, the South Pacific, the American Indians, and many others.

2. *Pitched instruments.* These are instruments that produce specific pitches and that are used for a variety of purposes in the general music class, including playing melodies, ostinati, chord roots, and chords.

a. *Melody percussion instruments,* including various types of tuned bar instruments and also small tympani. These are played with a variety of mallets and beaters.

b. *Keyboard instruments* used for non-complex classroom music activities. These include the standard piano and also other instruments, such as the many various types of organs and electronic pianos.

c. *Small wind instruments* belonging to the flute family and made of wood, plastic, or metal.

d. *Stringed instruments.* The standard instruments of the string family are often used in general music class activities. The most popular for this type of use are the string bass and the cello. Other instruments used include simplified traditional stringed instruments such as the gamba and the psaltery, which are constructed primarily for classroom use. In addition there are such stringed instruments as the autoharp and the ukulele, which children can use to play simple harmonic accompaniments for classroom music activities. It is also possible under certain circumstances to use the guitar and the mandolin in the general classroom for playing melodies or chords.

3. *The Orff instruments.* A special group of percussion instruments, which has recently come into wide use in elementary classrooms, is the group usually identified as the Orff instruments. These were created in connection with the work of the German composer, Carl Orff, as a result of experimentation with classes of children. A simplified statement of the beliefs about the instruments and the musical system in which they play such an important part might be stated thus:

a. Experience in rhythmic movement is a basic, fundamental requirement for musical growth, contributing to the ability to hear and understand music and to use musical rhythms in singing, playing, and dancing. Playing simple percussion instruments is one of the most satisfactory ways of providing this rhythmic experience for children. However, the child's own body is recognized as his first rhythm instrument. The Orff system includes a wide variety of activities, sometimes using free movements of the body and sometimes small, carefully articulated movements like those that involve the speech organs in connection with vocal chanting. (See section on chanting, page 22.) Movements used in bodily activity and in playing percussion instruments are closely correlated.

b. In addition to the rhythmic experience they have with instruments, children also need experience with pitched instruments. To be of the greatest value, such instruments should permit a child to start his musical activities comfortably, by playing the simplest of melodic motifs and to grow in skill at his own speed, developing his musical ear to recognize accuracy and variety in pitch and good quality in tone.

c. Children's development in musical skill is enhanced and deepened by creative activity in the use of both rhythm and pitched instruments.

d. Instruments for use in a classroom must be of excellent quality, with accurate pitch and musical tone quality, if they are to develop skill and taste in children.

With these ideas in mind, Carl Orff led the way in the production of a group of instruments bearing his name. These include rhythm instruments, which fall into the same groupings as the traditional instruments listed above: drums, tambourines, wood blocks, triangles, rattles, bells, cymbals, etc. An unique type of Orff percussion instrument is the set of small tympani for children. Like regular tympani, these are in several sizes and can be tuned. There is also a large group of Orff tuned bar melody percussion instruments in a variety of materials and pitches. These instruments are flexible, having removable bars, which can be arranged to include only those bars needed for a certain motif or ostinato the children are to play. They are called glockenspiels, xylophones, and metallophones. Some have bars of wood; some have metal bars. Some are high in pitch; others are low. Suggestions on the use of these instruments are found in Chapter 7 in the discussions of the use of tuned bar instruments.

The Orff teaching materials are listed on page 127. Since these materials were originally written for use in European situations, usually for classes of children in conservatories or special music schools, they require some study and adaptation to make them immediately useful in a general classroom. They are, however, worthy of study and can provide a wealth of ideas of tremendous value in developing musical consciousness and skill and the ability to hear, understand, and use both traditional and contemporary music. They begin with the simplest of instrumental parts, using the pentatonic scale at first and progressing to the use of all types of musical scales and harmonies. The great variety of additional material included in the way of chants, songs, and rhythmic activity can add excitement to the learning of music in any classroom.

5

Traditional
Rhythm Instruments
in the Classroom

A certain group of rhythm instruments came into popular use many years ago with the development of the school *rhythm band*, also called *percussion band* or *rhythm orchestra*. Such ensembles were usually considered to belong in the primary school: the kindergarten, the first grade, and possibly the second grade. At first they were considered performing groups, and sometimes they played from a printed musical score, each player having a special part for his instrument, which he learned by note or by rote, according to his skill.

During a later period, the emphasis was on informal playing of these instruments, and frequently an entire class played together in unison. This was regarded as a relaxation or fun activity, and all the instruments of all types pounded out the main accents in the music together without regard for secondary accents, the rhythm patterns, or the repetition and contrast to be found in the music.

Actually, rhythm instruments have no legitimate place in music education except as they serve a musical purpose. And they can serve such a purpose, not only in the primary grades, but also at any level where the learning of music fundamentals is taking place. Such learning includes the fundamental activities of hearing and feeling the swing, the beat, and the rhythm patterns in the music. It can also include the later experience of using music notation that pictures the swing, the beat and the rhythm patterns in either vocal or instrumental music. Rhythm instruments can also provide an enjoyable activity possible of adaptation to suit the interests of any age level and any type of group.

RHYTHM INSTRUMENTS: TYPES AND SELECTION

In the traditional rhythm or percussion bands and orchestras described above, most of the instruments used were small-sized percussion instruments, similar to those found in the percussion section of a standard orchestra: drums, tambourines, wood blocks, triangles, and cymbals. Through the years other instruments have been added to these. Rhythm sticks, jingle sticks, finger cymbals, jingle bells, sand blocks, rattles, and shakers are among those commonly used.

Although these instruments are sometimes sold in sets whose content is decided by the company from which they are purchased, many teachers prefer to select their own instruments, including those best suited to the needs of the children who will use them. This procedure also makes it possible for the teacher to select only good, well-constructed instruments that will produce a sound that is musical in quality and depth.

Primary Grades

Although the percussion instruments are seldom all played together in unison, it is valuable to have enough separate instruments available to provide one for each child in the group. This makes it possible for all to participate, even though they do not do so simultaneously.

Not all instruments are needed in equal quantities. Some are used for special effects only; some are so loud or so pentrating in sound that they must be used sparingly. A basic collection of instruments that can provide a varied musical experience in a lower grade class might include the following:

15 pairs of rhythm sticks	2 pairs of sand blocks
3 triangles	2 drums (2 sizes)
3 tambourines	3 rattles
4 wood blocks (2 sizes)	2 jingle sticks
2 pairs of cymbals	1 jingle bells
1 pair of finger cymbals	

Upper Grades

In line with the wider social and geographical interests and experiences of the intermediate and upper grades, the use of some of the folk-type rhythm instruments is important in these classes. The final choice of such instruments for classroom use will probably depend on the peoples and countries currently being studied by each class. (See page 63.) A relatively small number of the traditional school rhythm instruments is usually adequate at this level:

> 2 pairs of rhythm sticks
> 2 triangles (1 large, 1 small)
> 2 tambourines
> 2 wood blocks (2 sizes)
> 1 pair of cymbals
> 2 pairs of finger cymbals
> 2 drums (1 large hand drum, 1 tom-tom)

MAKING RHYTHM INSTRUMENTS

Substitutes for many of the traditional instruments listed above can be created for or by the children. In this connection it should be kept in mind that the quality of the instrument and of the sound it produces are of great importance, since the experience it provides is designed to be a musical one. For example, substitutes for cymbals should be made of metal heavy enough to give a musical ring; an instrument made of thin, tinny material can be used by the child to respond to the beat he hears in the music, but the sound produced will be so unmusical that much of the value of the activity will be lost.

Drums, too, can be made, and if the sound of the drum has depth and richness, it will be satisfactory regardless of the material from which it is constructed. If, however, the sound is dull and dead, the instrument will have little value in enriching a musical experience.

Horseshoes or large "ten-penny" nails can sometimes be used in place of triangles. Rice, tapioca, lead pellets, or pebbles enclosed in waxed ice cream cylinders, in small cans, or in mailing tubes can provide shakers with interesting variations in sound. Coconut shells can be made into substitutes for wood blocks.

Many suggestions for the making of rhythm instruments are to be found in the books listed in the bibliography at the end of this chapter. Chapter 6, on the use of folk and national instruments, includes additional ideas on instrument-making. With a little encouragement and guidance, the children's ingenuity, curiosity, and interest in experimentation will lead to the creation of many interesting, useful, and musically valuable classroom instruments.

CLASSROOM ACTIVITIES WITH RHYTHM INSTRUMENTS

Primary Grades

1. When introducing rhythm instruments to a lower grade class for the first time, it is usually desirable to present only one or two instruments at a time. Rhythm sticks are favorites for the first experiences.
2. Demonstrate the new instrument briefly for the class. If the sticks are being used, play them in time to the music, a stick in each hand. Steady march music is good, or a rhythmic song such as this one, sung by the class.

TEN LITTLE INDIANS

One lit - tle, two lit - tle, three lit - tle In - dians,

Four lit - tle, five lit - tle, six lit - tle In - dians,

Seven lit - tle, eight lit - tle, nine lit - tle In - dians,

Ten lit - tle In - dian boys.

3. Distribute the sticks to four or five children and repeat the activity. These children tap the sticks while the other children also move their arms in response to the rhythm. Children sitting on the floor or in little chairs usually tap the sticks alternately on the floor and together. Children sitting at tables or desks tap them on the desks and then together.

4. The sticks are passed to other children until everyone has had a chance to play them.

5. When the children are familiar with the sticks, introduce another instrument, preferably one with a very different sound—perhaps the triangle. Show the class how to hold and how to play the new instrument. It must be suspended from a cord or a holder when played. If a child holds the metal triangle in his hand as he strikes it, the sound will be deadened.

6. Gradually introduce the other instruments, encouraging the class to listen to the different sounds they produce. Play them to accompany suitable songs and recorded music. Many school music books include special songs for use in getting acquainted with each instrument separately: sticks, triangle, drum, tambourine, etc.

7. One of the things that makes this type of activity valuable to children is the fact that a different kind of physical movement is required for the playing of each instrument. A child may find one of these movements easy, another difficult. He needs to be allowed to try each instrument as it is introduced, and this will require planning on the part of the teacher.

8. It is important to begin at once to help the children to become sensitive to the different sounds of the instruments, and their possible uses with music. For example, with a familiar song like "Five Little Chickadees," the children listen to decide where the triangle might best fit. Usually they will suggest the refrain, "Chickadee, chickadee," etc. Perhaps the sticks can be played on the verse and the triangle on the refrain, and this can provide a beginning in the understanding of the uses of the various instruments.

FIVE LITTLE CHICKADEES

1. Five   lit - tle   chick - a - dees,   peep-ing   at   the   door;
2. Four   lit - tle   chick - a - dees,   sit - ing   in   a   tree;

One   flew   a - way   and   then   there   were   four.
One   flew   a - way   and   then   there   were   three.

Refrain

Chick - a - dee,   chick - a - dee,   hap - py   and   gay;

Chick - a - dee,   chick - a - dee,   fly   a - way.

3. Three little chickadees,
   Looking at you,
   One flew away
   And then there were two.

4. Two little chickadees,
   Sitting in the sun,
   One flew away
   And then there was one.

5. One little chickadee,
   Left all alone,
   It flew away
   And then there was none.

From *Growing With Music, Teachers Edition, Book 1.* © 1966 by Prentice-Hall, Inc.

9. When all of the instruments are familiar, use each of them often but not continually. Instead of having them all played at once, help boys and girls to make them "speak" as distinctive voices whenever they are heard. They should be used as musical instruments and not as noisemakers! An excellent dramatization in which rhythm instruments are used thus distinctively is "A Zoo Tale" in *Rhythms Today!* (See bibliography at the end of this chapter.)

Upper Grades

While the following activities are suggested for the upper grades, sometimes the children at the primary grade level can participate in them without difficulty. If these older children cannot yet play such instruments in time to the rhythm of the music, or have not learned to use the various sounds musically and with discrimination, they will profit from experiences such as those listed above. It will be important in this case to make sure the songs used are suitable to the age level of the children.

1. Using rhythm sticks or a wood block, the teacher plays a short rhythm pattern such as: ♩ ♫♩ ♩ ♩ | ♩ ♩ ♩ ♩ . The class repeats what was heard, playing the sticks or tapping their fingers lightly. This continues with a variety of simply organized patterns of this kind played and repeated without a break between the pattern and the answer if possible. This is done entirely by ear and without the use of notes. For other suggestions for this type of activity, see page 17.
2. Rhythm instruments can be used to accompany chants of names, words, jingles, and rhymes. See page 22.
3. When new rhythm patterns and note values are introduced in the later grades, the rhythm instruments will prove very helpful in developing a clear feeling for the sound and the physical movement connected with each pattern or note. New and familiar rhythm patterns can be presented on charts or flash cards. The teacher plays one pattern from among several shown. The class identifies it and plays it, watching the notes and using rhythm instruments. A member of the class chooses a pattern to be played by the class. Sometimes they chant the rhythm as they play, and sometimes they step the notes while playing.

The same kind of activity can be carried on with music from the books used by the class. The rhythm notation of a song with familiar note values can be played, using percussion instruments. Many different variations of this type of activity or of games developed from it can be enjoyed, and the children will increase in skill in following the notes smoothly and intelligently in so far as the rhythm notation is concerned.

A familiar round such as "Are You Sleeping?" can be accompanied by percussion instruments. The instruments are divided into as many contrasting groups as there are groups singing the round. For example, Group I can play rhythm sticks and wood blocks; Group II, rattles; Group III, jingle bells and tambourines; Group IV, triangles and finger cymbals. As each group begins its part in the song, they also play their instruments. It is important that the tempo of the song be slow enough to allow the children not only to sing and play but also to *hear* the several parts together and the interweaving of long and short notes.

Sources on
Traditional Rhythm
Instruments: Making
and Using Them

Books

Andrews, Gladys, *Creative Rhythmic Movement for Children.* Englewood Cliffs, N.J.: Prentice-Hall, Inc., 1954.

Barr, Lawrence, Elizabeth Blair, Walter Ehret, *You and Music.* Englewood Cliffs, N.J.: Prentice-Hall, Inc., 1959.

Clemens, James R., *Invitation to Rhythm.* Dubuque, Iowa: Wm. C. Brown Company, Publishers, 1962.

Coleman, Satis, *Creative Music in the Home.* Valparaiso, Ind.: Lewis E. Myers and Co., 1927.

————, *The Drum Book.* New York: The John Day Company, Inc., 1931.

Doll, Edna, and Mary Jarman Nelson, *Rhythms Today!* Morristown, N.J.: Silver Burdett Company, 1965. Records available.

Ellison, Alfred, *Music with Children.* New York: McGraw-Hill Book Company, 1959.

Garretson, Robert L., *Music in Childhood Education.* New York: Appleton-Century-Crofts, 1966.

Krone, Beatrice P., and Kurt R. Miller, *Help Yourselves to Music* (2nd ed.). Belmont, Calif.: Wadsworth Publishing Company, Inc., 1968.

Mandell, Muriel, and Robert E. Wood, *Make Your Own Musical Instruments.* New York: Sterling Publishing Co., 1957.

Mason, Bernard S., *Drums, Tomtoms and Rattles.* New York: A. S. Barnes & Co., 1938.

Myers, Louise K., *Teaching Children Music in the Elementary School* (3rd ed.). Englewood Cliffs, N.J.: Prentice-Hall, Inc., 1961.

Nelson, Mary Jarman, and Gladys Tipton, *Music for Early Childhood.* Morristown, N.J.: Silver Burdett Company, 1952.

Nye, Robert E., and Vernice T. Nye, *Music in the Elementary School* (3rd ed.). Englewood Cliffs, N.J.: Prentice-Hall, Inc., 1970.

Rainbow, Bernarr, ed., *Handbook for Music Teachers,* Book I. London: Novello and Co. Ltd., 1964.

Runkle, Aleta, and Mary LeBow Eriksen, *Music for Today's Boys and Girls.* Boston: Allyn & Beacon, Inc., 1966.

Sheehy, Emma D., *Children Discover Music and Dance.* New York: Holt, Rinehart & Winston, Inc., 1959.

Slind, Lloyd H., and D. Evan Davis, *Bringing Music To Children.* New York: Harper & Row, Publishers, 1964.

Snyder, Alice M., *Creating Music With Children*. New York: Mills Music, Inc., 1957.

Surplus, Robert, *The Beat of the Drum*. Minneapolis: Lerner Publications Company, 1963.

Swanson, Bessie R., *Music in the Education of Children* (3rd ed.). Belmont, Calif.: Wadsworth Publishing Company, Inc., 1969. Also, handbook: *Planning Music in the Education of Children*, 1965.

Records

"Let's Have a Rhythm Band" from *Let's Play a Musical Game*. Columbia Harmony Records, LP 9522.

6

Folk and National
Rhythm Percussion
Instruments

Most of the peoples of the world have their own native percussion instruments, which they use to provide music for songs and dances. Some of these are rhythm percussion instruments, while others are percussion instruments that are used to produce special musical effects, sometimes melodic or harmonic rather than rhythmic. This chapter is concerned primarily with the *rhythm percussion instruments*.

The rhythms produced by these instruments constitute an important part of the traditional music of the countries from which they come. Boys and girls today need to develop an understanding of the people in different parts of the world. Acquaintance with the instruments, songs, and dances can contribute greatly to such an understanding.

It is impossible in the space available here to list all the folk or national percussion instruments that could be used profitably in the classroom. Only a very few examples can be included, representing a few of the peoples and geographical areas of interest to children. Some of the percussion instruments suggested below would, in a native situation, be used in combination with melody or harmony instruments, while in other situations they would be used alone. Some of the ways of using folk and national rhythm percussion instruments are relatively uncomplicated and not too difficult for children. Much of the music played by folk and national melody and harmony instruments, however, is complex. For this reason most of the attention in these pages is given to rhythm percussion instruments.

AMERICAN INDIAN
PERCUSSION INSTRUMENTS

Music of the American Indian, particularly dance music, has been (and is today) accompanied and often directed by percussion instruments, among which are the following types:

Tom-tom. This is a drum of medium size with a hard drum head. It is beaten either with a stick or with the hand. Tom-toms for use in the school are available in various sizes. Since increasing the size lowers the pitch, most classes enjoy the variety in pitch produced by instruments of at least two contrasting sizes. Following are some classroom activities in which the tom-tom can be used:

1. Play a steady beat to accompany a slow, shuffling dance around a circle (♩ ♩ ♩ ♩). Aside from the dramatic aspects of this type of activity, it has value in helping children, even very small children, to hear a steady, recurring beat without the confusion caused by a variety of other sounds. The child can *hear* the beat clearly and this may help him to adapt his movements to fit it. Most of the recorded music we use for classroom rhythmic activity includes so many different rhythm patterns simultaneously that the small child may become confused in his response.

2. Play a steady beat for a faster dance, perhaps with hopping steps. This may be for a (pseudo) war dance or festival celebration

3. Combine these two patterns to accompany a dance or a song such as the following. Use two different tom-toms, a large one for the slow beat (quarter notes) and a smaller one for the fast beats (eighth notes).

INDIAN DANCE SONG

Hi   yo,   hi yo ip see   nee yah,   hi   yo;   Hi yo ip see

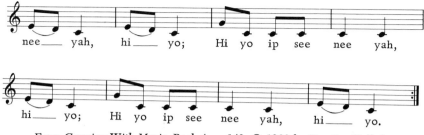

nee___ yah,   hi___ yo;   Hi yo ip see   nee   yah,

hi___ yo;   Hi yo ip see   nee   yah,   hi___ yo.

From *Growing With Music*, Book 4, p. 142. © 1966 by Prentice-Hall, Inc.

4. Use the tom-tom to send messages. Chant out the accented and un-accented syllables of a simple repeated message, and then accompany the chant on the tom-tom. Classes that have already learned to use rhythm notation can use it with the chants; others can simply play the rhythm of the words by ear. Small dialogues can be chanted and played on the tom-tom by individuals. For example:

" Where are you ? Where are you ? "

" In the for - est, in the for - est. "

" Hur - ry home, hur - ry home "   etc.

The recording "Little Indian Drum" (Young People's Records 15006) has special value in this kind of activity.

Large drum. A large, deep-toned drum, probably covered by heavy skin, can be used to accompany dances and songs, as was suggested above for the tom-tom. A group of players will often kneel around the drum, all of them playing it. Sometimes they strike the drum with the right hand and play a rattle with the left.

Rattles. Each Indian tribe has its own types of rattles. There are deer hoof rattles and gourd rattles, which are shaken by the players. There are also strings of shells (seashells, turtle shells, nut shells) worn on thongs around the ankles of the dancers or held in the hands.

Bells. The jingling of small bells plays an important part in many kinds of Indian dance music. Strings of small bells may be fastened around parts of the body, ankles, wrist, or waist, to jingle with the dancer's movements.

Sources on
Indian Percussion
Instruments

Books

Bauer, Marion, and Ethel R. Peyser, *Music Through the Ages* (edited and revised by Elizabeth E. Rogers). New York: G. P. Putnam's Sons, 1967.

Coleman, Satis, *Creative Music in the Home.* Valparaiso, Ind.: Lewis E. Myers and Co., 1927.

————, *The Drum Book.* New York: The John Day Company, Inc., 1931.

Edgerly, Beatrice, *From the Hunter's Bow.* New York: G. P. Putnam's Sons, 1942.

Gale, Albert, Max Krone, and Beatrice Krone, *Songs and Stories of the American Indians.* Park Ridge, Ill.: Neil A. Kjos Music Company, Publisher, 1949.

Goodin, Virginia, *Sounds of the Lake and the Forest.* Hillsdale, Mich.: Hillsdale Educational Publishers, Inc., 1960.

Hofmann, Charles, *War Whoops and Medicine Songs.* Boston: The Boston Music Company, 1952.

Kurath, Gertrude P., *Michigan Indian Festivals.* Ann Arbor, Mich.: Ann Arbor Publishers, 1966.

Mason, Bernard S., *Dances and Stories of the American Indian.* New York: A. S. Barnes & Co., 1944.

————, *Drums, Tomtoms and Rattles.* New York: A. S. Barnes & Co., 1937.

Tooze, Ruth, and Beatrice P. Krone, *Literature and Music as Resources for the Social Studies.* Englewood Cliffs, N.J.: Prentice-Hall, Inc., 1955.

Records

"Chant of the Eagle Dancers," *Music of American Indians.* RCA Victor, E89.

Folk Instruments of the World. Follett Publishing Company, Album L24.

(The) Great Plains Indian Singers and Songs. Canyon Records ARP 6052.

Indian Music of the Southwest. Recorded by Laura Bolton. Folkways, FW 8850.

Music of the American Indian. Library of Congress, AAFS L34–43. Ten records of music of various tribes. Percussion instruments accompany much of the music.

(The) Song of the Indian. Canyon Records C6050.

Elementary Music Series Books

Indian songs with percussion instrument accompaniment: "Navajo Happy Song," *Discovering Music Together,* Book 5; "Snake-Dance Song," *The Magic of Music,* Book 4; *"Corn-Grinding Song," Exploring Music 3 (Music for Young Americans,* Book 3); *"Canoe Song," Growing With Music,* Book 3; "Song of the Needlefish," *This Is Music,* Book 4; "Navaho Happy Song," *Exploring Music,* Book 3; "Breezes Are Blowing," *Making Music Your Own,* Book 3; "Desert Fruit," *Music in Our Country (Music for Living,* Book 5); "Sahuaro Legend Song," *Music Across Our Country (Together We Sing,* Book 4); "Morning Song," *Music for Young Americans,* Book 7.

LATIN AMERICAN
RHYTHM INSTRUMENTS

Much of the indigenous music of Latin America features unique and distinctive percussion instruments, some of which are rhythm instruments, while others produce melody and harmony. Only the use of the rhythm instruments in the classroom is discussed here.

Children who are studying about life in the Latin American countries will be interested to learn songs and dances originating here, and the color provided by the folk instruments with their characteristic sounds and rhythms will add appreciably to the experience.

In this connection it is important to give considerable attention to the native music of Puerto Rico. Puerto Rican music is closely related in style and instruments to the typical music of other Latin American areas. Since this island is American, and since there are great numbers of Puerto Ricans living on the mainland, it is important to develop familiarity with and respect for this music.

Because of the complexity of some of the rhythm patterns used in this native music and the skill required to play many of the instruments, any extensive activity with these instruments is usually more successful in the middle and upper grades than in the primary grades. Some of the true Latin American rhythms are too complex to be played in their original form by elementary school children and must be simplified. Most of these rhythms can be learned by rote from hearing the teacher play or by listening to a recording. This approach is better than an attempt to read the complicated rhythm notation of much of the music.

Types of Instruments
and Their Uses

In most school situations, only a few instruments of this type are needed. The sound of the instrument is often very penetrating, and the effect will be more musical and more true to the original music if very few of any one kind are used in the accompaniments for songs or dances. All of the children in the group should have the opportunity to try all of the instruments, but not all of them should be played at the same time continually. Introduce the instruments one at a time so that the sound and the characteristic rhythm patterns of each can be clearly heard and recognized.

The following types of Latin American instruments are of special value in the elementary school classroom.

Drums. From among many types of drums, some of the most popular for classroom use are:

1. Large keg drums, deep in tone, frequently made from a nail keg or a small barrel.
2. Bongo drums, small drums, higher in pitch than the large ones, and usually used in groups of two or three, in various sizes and pitches.
3. Conga drums, tall and narrow, played with hands or with a beater.

The large drum plays the steady basic beat in the music, while the other instruments, including the bongo and conga drums, play the more florid, complex parts, which are often syncopated. The bongo drum is very versatile, and offers many possibilities for variety in sound. All of these drums produce one kind of sound and effect when they are struck on the rim and another when played in the center. They can be played with sticks or beaters but also produce a great variety of sounds when the hand is used. They are slapped with flat fingers, struck with the "heel" of the hand, or played with fingers, which tap or slide. Sometimes both hands play on one drum, shifting from rim to center, in response to the music. Again, the two hands play on two different drums, producing a duet or dialogue.

Natives of the West Indian islands construct metal drums from empty oil barrels and tune them to produce the fascinating music of the famous steel bands—music that is melodic and harmonic as well as rhythmic. These instruments have a deep ringing tone and are played with a large soft beater.

Maracas. These are colorful gourd rattles that are found in the Latin American dance band. Frequently they play an even, steady rhythm: ♫ ♫ ♫ ♫. Sometimes they play an uneven rhythm such as ♩. ♪♩ ♩ or a syncopated rhythm like this: ♪♩ ♪♩ ♩

Many children enjoy making their own gourd maracas. Here are some suggestions for such a project:

1. Allow the gourd to dry thoroughly and in natural (not artificially heated) air over a long period of time.

2. Make small openings in the top and bottom of the gourd and remove membranes and seeds.
3. Brush the inside of the thoroughly dry gourd with a shellac which will dry to form a hard surface.
4. Experiment with various materials for the rattle, such as rice, lead shot, tapioca, beans, and pebbles.
5. Add a handle, preferably one that goes through and out of the top of the gourd. Plastic wood can be used to seal the holes.
6. Use color and design to decorate the rattles. Much Latin American folk art is beautiful, interesting, and understandable to children in its form and color.

Guiro. The guiro is a long gourd with a series of deep, sharp grooves cut into its surface. A "scratcher," usually made of two strands of heavy wire fastened to a handle is drawn across the grooves, producing a sharp, rapid, clicking sound. A stick may also be used as a "scratcher." The instrument plays various rhythm patterns. A favorite is: ♩. ♪ ♩ ♩. Sometimes a notched stick is used in place of the gourd and is scratched to produce the clicking rhythms described above.

Claves. The claves are resonating wooden bars that produce a loud, sharp sound important in Latin American music. It requires a great deal of skill to hold and strike the claves as professional players do. Children usually simply strike one bar on the other. The rhythm patterns played by the instrument are often complex, and most of them are best learned by rote, perhaps from a record. A good wood block will make a satisfactory substitute for the claves in classroom music activities.

Castanets. Like the claves, true castanets are not easy instruments to play and require a great deal of practice. Castanets on a stick are available, however, and are not difficult to play. They are often used not only in the elementary school classroom but also in dance bands and symphony orchestras. The castanets are particularly important as a means of adding a kind of native flavor to certain types of dance music.

Cabassa. This is a large colorful gourd around which there is a loose netting on which wooden beads are strung. The instrument is used to provide rhythms similar to those produced by the maracas.

Miscellaneous. Latin American music offers a wide variety of unique instrumental effects and each country adds its own special touches. Some other instruments of importance are: *Chocallo,* a long tube with rattles inside, held in both hands and shaken back and forth to produce a rhythmic sound; *tambourine;* and *cowbell,* used chiefly for points of special emphasis in the music.

Sources on
Latin American
Instruments and Their
Use in the Classroom

Books

Brandão, Jose Bieira, Max Krone, and Beatrice Krone, *Folksongs of Brazil.* Park Ridge, Ill.: Neil A. Kjos Music Company, Publisher, 1947.

Clemens, James R., *Invitation to Rhythm.* Dubuque, Iowa: Wm. C. Brown Company, Publishers, 1962.

Krone, Beatrice, and Max Krone, *Inter-Americana.* Park Ridge, Ill.: Neil A. Kjos Music Company, Publisher, 1945.

————, and Kurt R. Miller, *Help Yourselves to Music* (2nd ed.). Belmont, Calif.: Wadsworth Publishing Company, Inc., 1968.

Krugman, Lillian D., and Alice Jeanne Ludwig, *Little Calypsos.* Far Rockaway, N.Y.: Carl Van Roy Co., 1955.

McLaughlin, Roberta, and Bessie Mae Stanchfield, *Cancioncitas.* Minneapolis: Schmitt, Hall & McCreary, 1948.

Millan, Amalia, Beatrice Krone, and Max Krone, *Folksongs of Mexico.* Park Ridge, Ill.: Neil A. Kjos Music Company, Publisher, 1948.

Morales, Humbert, *Latin American Rhythm Instruments.* New York: H. Adler Publishers Corp., 1954.

Perry, Sylvia, and Lillian D. Krugman, *Song Tales of the West Indies.* Far Rockaway, N.Y.: Carl Van Roy Co., 1964.

Swanson, Bessie R., *Music in the Education of Children* (3rd ed.). Belmont, Calif.: Wadsworth Publishing Company, Inc., 1969.

Tooze, Ruth, and Beatrice Perham Krone, *Literature and Music as Resources for Social Studies.* Englewood Cliffs, N.J.: Prentice-Hall, Inc., 1955.

Records

Brazilian Songs for Children. Carl Van Roy Co., CVR 704R.

Children's Songs of Mexico. Bowmar Records, Inc., Album 147.

Folk Instruments of the World. Follett Publishing Company, Album L24.

Multi-Media Kit: Mexico. International Communication Films. Instruments, sound-color filmstrips, and miscellaneous artifacts are included.

Toccata for Percussion, Third Movement, Chavez. Columbia 5847.

Elementary Music Series Books

Puerto Rican songs with rhythm instrument accompaniment: "La calle ancha," *Making Music Your Own,* Book 4; "Los tres Santos Reyes," *Making Music*

Your Own, Book 5; "Bonita," *Music in Our Country (Music for Living,* Book 5); "Dancing the Merengue," *This Is Music,* Book 3.

Miscellaneous Latin American songs with rhythm instrument accompaniment. "Pirulito," *The Magic of Music,* Book 4; "The Son of the Count," *This Is Music,* Book 5; "Carmen Carmela," *Growing With Music,* Book 6; "In Bahia Town," *Discovering Music Together,* Book 3; "South of the Border," *Understanding Music (Music for Young Americans,* Book 4); "All Hail the Queen," *Making Music Your Own,* Book 6; "Tinga Layo," *Exploring Music,* Book 3; "Samba-lele," *Voices of the World (Together We Sing,* Book 6); "The Green Hills," *Music Near and Far (Music for Living,* Book 4); "Angelico," *Music for Young Americans,* Book 8; "Baizhan Boy," *Discovering Music Together,* Book 7.

AFRICAN NATIVE
RHYTHM INSTRUMENTS

African Drums

Each of Africa's many nations has its own unique drums, and it is not possible to use or study all of them in the classroom. Some activity with instruments of this type will, however, capture the imagination of children. From among the many kinds of drums, the following are suggested for possible use in the elementary school: the large hollow log drums (which have no drumheads); the tree trunk drums; the hourglass-shaped drum, called the "dundun" in some African countries; various other drums, some of which are like the tom-tom and the conga drum of the Americas. Some of these drums have one head, but many have a tightly stretched drumhead at each end. They are sometimes played with the hands, but more often with a wooden beater that has a curved head. Drums are often given names by the players.

An African orchestra or drum choir will have drums of various sizes, pitches and "voices" (light, big, etc.). African drums have a variety of uses. They are used as talking drums, which send messages; they are important in special ceremonies; they accompany dances. A fascinating classroom activity that makes special use of the drums is the sending of messages on the so-called talking drums. All kinds of messages are sent by this native telegraph system. After children have read or heard about some of these countries, they will enjoy creating messages to chant and sound out on the drums:

" Hun - ter com - ing. . . . . "   ♩   ♩   ♩   ♩

" Find the wa - ter buf - fa - lo. . . . . "   ♫ ♫ ♫ ♩

Many African orchestras also include xylophones of different sizes and types. The simplest of these plays only one note and is made of a single slab of wood, which is put across two small tree trunks.

Rhythmic Accompaniments for African Songs and Dances

The use of the body as a percussion instrument is important in African music; stamping and clapping in many different ways provide a steady rhythm. In addition to the drums, a variety of other instruments is heard, particularly in dance music: gourd rattles, clapping sticks, and many kinds of small bells and rattles worn on the ankles, around the neck, and as bracelets by the dancers.

Children can learn a great deal about native African music from books and pictures and from listening to recordings. There are other fascinating African musical instruments, both rhythmic and melodic, in addition to those mentioned above. Many of them give evidence of a rich, old, and often sophisticated musical culture.

Sources on African Rhythm Instruments and Their Use in the Classroom

Books

Beal, Newton, *Pygmies Are People.* Far Rockaway, N.Y.: Carl Van Roy Co., 1964.

Coleman, Satis, *The Drum Book.* New York: The John Day Company, Inc., 1931.

Dietz, Betty Warned, and Michael Babatunde Olatunji, *Musical Instruments of Africa.* New York: The John Day Company, Inc., 1965. Book and record.

Doll, Edna, and Mary Jarman Nelson, *Rhythms Today!* Morristown, N.J.: Silver Burdett Company, 1965.

Edgerly, Beatrice, *From the Hunter's Bow.* New York: G. P. Putnam's Sons, 1942.

Hughes, Langston, *The First Book of Africa.* New York: Franklin Watts, 1960.

Landeck, Beatrice, *Echoes of Africa in Folk Songs of the Americas.* New York: David McKay Co., Inc., 1961.

Malm, William P., *Music Cultures of the Pacific, the Near East, and Asia.* Englewood Cliffs, N.J.: Prentice-Hall, Inc., 1966.

Nye, Vernice T., Robert E. Nye, and H. Virginia Nye, *Toward World Understanding With Song*. Belmont, Calif.: Wadsworth Publishing Company, Inc., 1967.

Rohrbough, Lynn, *African Song Sampler*. Delaware, Ohio: Cooperative Recreation Service, 1958.

Sachs, Kurt. *History of Musical Instruments*. New York: W. W. Norton & Company, Inc., 1940.

Tooze, Ruth and Beatrice P. Krone. *Literature and Music as Resources for Social Studies*. Englewood Cliffs, N.J.: Prentice-Hall, Inc., 1955.

Records

African and Afro-American Drums, Vol. 1. Ethnic Folkways, FE 4502.

African Music. Laura Bolton. Ethnic Folkways, FW 8852.

Music of Africa. Gallotone, Galp 1041.

Music of the Cameroons. Ethnic Folkways, FE 4372.

Music of the Dan. From UNESCO Collection, *An Anthology of African Music*, 2301. Bärenreiter Musicaphon.

Songs and Sounds of Faraway Places. Philips, PCC 601.

World Library of Folk and Primitive Music, Vol. 2, *French Africa*. Columbia SL205.

Elementary Music Series Books

African songs with rhythm instrument accompaniment: "Kokolioko," *This Is Music*, Book 4; "Before Dinner," *Discovering Music Together*, Book 6; "Jungle Drums," *Exploring Music (Music for Young Americans*, Book 3); "The Peacock," *Making Music Your Own*, Book 6; "Saturday Night," *Exploring Music*, Book 6; "Kum Ba Yah," *Growing With Music*, Book 6; "The Jog Trot," *Music Near and Far (Music for Living*, Book 4); "Sizinyoni," *Music for Young Americans*, Book 8; "Allunde," *Discovering Music Together*, Book 7.

PERCUSSION INSTRUMENTS OF THE ASIAN PACIFIC COUNTRIES

All of the Asian countries bordering on the Pacific and many of the Pacific islands have their own unique dances and songs. Percussion instruments are important in the' musical groups that accompany the singing and dancing. Boys and girls in our schools are interested to hear the various sounds produced by these instruments, to see pictures or films of them, and to see and hear them in concert whenever possible. They can begin to develop an understanding of some of the widely varied cultures of the modern world if, for example, they have the opportunity to get acquainted with the sound of an Indonesian *gamelan* (orchestra) and to compare it with the sound of music that is more familiar, perhaps that of an American square dance orchestra or a Mexican folk orchestra. This beginning should be followed by some study of the countries and by further experience with their music, dances, and costumes. If an ethnomusicologist is available to give an illustrated lecture about the music of any of these peoples, this will be interesting and valuable in an elementary school.

The following pages of brief discussions of elementary classroom study of Asian Pacific countries and their music include these topics: "Indonesian Gamelan Percussion Instruments"; "Traditional Percussion Instruments of China"; "Korean Music and Percussion Instruments"; "Japanese Music and Percussion Instruments"; "Rhythm Percussion Instruments of the Philippines."

The books listed below are suggested as sources of information on musical instruments of many of the Asian Pacific countries. Recordings and music from the individual countries are listed with the section on each country.

Bauer, Marion, and Ethel R. Peyser, *Music Through the Ages* (edited and revised by Elizabeth E. Rogers). New York: G. P. Putnam's Sons, 1967.

Edgerly, Beatrice, *From the Hunter's Bow*. New York: G. P. Putnam's Sons, 1942.

Krone, Beatrice P., and Kurt R. Miller, *Help Yourselves to Music* (2nd ed.). Belmont, Calif.: Wadsworth Publishing Company, Inc., 1968.

Malm, William P., *Japanese Music and Musical Instruments*. Rutland, Vt.: E. Tuttle Co., 1959.

————, *Music Cultures of the Pacific, Near East, and Asia*. Englewood Cliffs, N.J.: Prentice-Hall, Inc., 1967.

Sachs, Kurt, *History of Musical Instruments*. New York: W. W. Norton & Company, Inc., 1940.

Tooze, Ruth, and Beatrice P. Krone. *Literature and Music as Resources for Social Studies*. Englewood Cliffs, N.J.: Prentice-Hall, Inc., 1955.

INDONESIAN GAMELAN
PERCUSSION INSTRUMENTS

A gamelan is a unique native orchestra found in Indonesia, particularly in Java and Bali. Children in the elementary school classroom will enjoy getting acquainted with the instruments of the gamelan and the metallic ring of the music they produce. Just as the music played by concert or dance orchestras in our part of the world is not suitable for performance by boys and girls, so also the music of the gamelan, as played by native groups, is too complex for elementary school classes to learn. As they become familiar with the sound of the music, however, the understanding the children have of the instruments and of this new musical idiom will be increased if they have an opportunity to play some instruments of this type. For example, very effective simple accompaniments can be played for folksongs from this section of the Pacific.

A gamelan is really a percussion orchestra, and it includes many types of xylophones, and also different kinds of cymbals, drums, gongs, and chimes. Some of the drums are made of wood, with drum heads of skin; they may be played with the hands or with a wooden beating stick. Other drums are of bronze and are of many sizes, from very small to large. Most of the instruments are mounted to allow nothing to interfere with the resonance and vibration. Some hang upright and some rest horizontally on stretched cords.

After listening carefully to some of the recorded music of these orchestras and reading about them, children can profitably experiment with playing a few carefully selected instruments of this type. Teachers will be interested in the article, "Improvisation as a Discipline in Javanese Music" by Mantle Hood, found in the *Music Educators Journal*, February–March, 1964.

Records of Gamelan Music

Folk Instruments of the World. Follett Publishing Company, Album L24.

(The) History of Music in Sound, Vol. I, Ancient and Oriental Music. RCA Victor, LM6057.

Music of the Orient. Decca, D 107.

Music of the World's Peoples, Vol. I. Ethnic Folkways, 4504.

Songs and Sounds of Faraway Places. Philips, PCC 601.

World Library of Folk and Primitive Music, Vol. 7, Indonesian Music. Columbia, KL210.

Elementary Music Series Books

Songs to which accompaniments by some of the gamelan instruments can be added: "In Surabaya," *Discovering Music Together,* Book 6; "Suliram," *Making Music Your Own,* Book 6; "Gambangan" and "Suliram," *Exploring Music,* Book 6; "In Surabaya," *Voices of the World* (*Together We Sing,* Book 6).

TRADITIONAL PERCUSSION
INSTRUMENTS OF CHINA

Percussion instruments have always been used to accompany the traditional songs, dances and operas of the Chinese people. According to ancient beliefs, there were considered to be eight sound-producing materials for instruments: skin, stone, metal, clay or baked earth, wood, bamboo, silk and gourd. As is true in traditional Chinese art, so in music also, emphasis is given and ideas are conveyed through careful selection of line and color, rather than through a profusion of detail or a large number of instruments playing together. Each instrument is used to produce a particular and unique effect and to emphasize a special dramatic idea. Percussion instruments are usually used in orchestras that also include melody instruments belonging to the wind and string families.

Chinese percussion instruments of special value in the activities of the elementary classroom include drums, gongs of wood, metal, or stone, temple blocks or wood blocks, large cymbals and finger cymbals, clappers and rattles, tambourines, and bells. These are usually most effective in a classroom when a few at a time are used in song accompaniments.

Records of Traditional Chinese Instrumental Music

Chinese Classical Instrumental Music. Ethnic Folkways, FW6812.
Chinese Drums and Gongs. Lyric 7102.
Folk Instruments of the World. Follett Publishing Company, Album L24.
Music of the Orient. Decca, DX 107.
Music of the World's Peoples, Vol. 2. Ethnic Folkways, 4505.

Elementary Music Series Books

Chinese songs with percussion instrument accompaniments: "The Narcissus," *This Is Music,* Book 3; "After School," *The Magic of Music,* Book 3; "Fengyang Drum," *Discovering Music Together,* Book 6; "Lovely New Year Flower," *Growing With Music,* Book 3; "Feng Yang Song," *Making Music Your Own,* Book 6; "How chun kok," *Exploring Music,* Book 5; "In China," *Exploring Music (Music for Young Americans,* Book 3); "Song of the Hoe," *Voices of the World (Together We Sing,* Book 6); "Lotus Blossoms," *Discovering Music Together,* Book 7; "The Purple Bamboo," *Exploring Music,* Book 6.

KOREAN MUSIC AND PERCUSSION INSTRUMENTS

The music of Korea is closely related to the music of China, but it has its own individual styles and sounds. Percussion instruments used with native Korean music include drums of many types, cymbals, triangles, bells, rattles, and several kinds of wood block instruments. These, with stringed instruments and many types of wind instruments make up the Korean orchestra.

Records of Korean Instrumental Music

Korea, Vocal and Instrumental Music. Ethnic Folkways, FE 4325.
Folk Instruments of the World. Follett Publishing Company, Album L24.
Music of the World's Peoples, Vol. 4. Ethnic Folkways, 4507.
World Library of Folk and Primitive Music, Vol. II, Japan, the Ryukyus, Formosa and Korea. Columbia SL214.

Elementary Music Series Books

Korean songs using percussion instrument accompaniment: "Toraji," *Growing With Music,* Book 6; "Arirang," *Exploring Music,* Book 6; "The Willow Trees," *This Is Music,* Book 6; "Song of Bluebells," "Ahrirang," *Discovering Music Together,* Book 6.

JAPANESE MUSIC AND PERCUSSION INSTRUMENTS

Melody instruments such as the *koto* and the *samisen* are much used in traditional Japanese music, sometimes almost to the exclusion of the percussion instruments. Percussion instruments are used especially for dance music and for music that accompanies dramatic productions; they are important for enhancing dramatic effects.

Many Japanese percussion instruments are very similar in type to those of China and Korea. They include many kinds of drums: huge drums played with heavy lacquered beaters, producing the heavy beats in dance music; small drums suspended from stands and struck with sticks; horizontal drums with two drum heads, so constructed that the pitch can be raised or lowered. The smaller drums set the rhythm patterns for the dances, and added points of emphasis are produced by the players, who shout at certain spots in the music as they play.

Many sizes of gongs are used in Japan; most of these are made of brass and are struck with hard tipped sticks. In addition to the gongs, the orchestras include chimes, rattles, bells, large cymbals and finger cymbals, wood blocks or temple blocks of differing pitches, and sticks that are struck together much as the Latin American claves are played. The true rhythms played by the Japanese musicians seem extremely complex to adults as well as to boys and girls who are not familiar with them. Children will, however, enjoy hearing this music, and a few instruments of this type can be used effectively to accompany some of the Japanese songs sung by the class.

Sources on
Japanese Music and
Percussion Instruments

Books

Malm, William P., *Japanese Music and Musical Instruments*. Rutland, Vt.: E. Tuttle Co., 1959.

White, Florence, and Kazuo Akiyama, *Children's Songs from Japan*. New York: Edward B. Marks Music Corp., 1960.

Records

Folk Instruments of the World. Follett Publishing Company, Album L24.

Japanese Temple Music. Lyrichord, LL117.

(A) *Musical Anthology of the Orient*. From UNESCO Collection. Bärenreiter Muscaphon, BM 30L2013.

Music of the World's Peoples, Vol. 1. Ethnic Folkways, 4504.

World Library of Folk and Primitive Music, Vol. II, Japan, the Ryukyus, Formosa, and Korea. Columbia SL214.

Elementary Music Series Books

Japanese songs with percussion instrument accompaniment: "Teru, Teru, Bozu," *Making Music Your Own*, Book 3; "Cherry Blossoms," *The Magic of Music*,

Book 4; "Koto and Tsuzumi," *Exploring Music*, Book 4; "Dragonflies," *Understanding Music* (*Music for Young Americans*, Book 4); "Cherry Blooms," *Discovering Music Together*, Book 6; "Coal Miner's Song," *Music Around the World* (*Music for Living*, Book 6); "Cherry Blooms," *Voices of the World* (*Together We Sing*, Book 6).

RHYTHM PERCUSSION INSTRUMENTS OF THE PHILIPPINES

Many melody- and harmony-producing instruments of different kinds, including flutes and stringed instruments (chiefly those played by plucking), together with a variety of percussion instruments, are used in the native music of the Philippines. The *rondallo*, a favorite native string ensemble is made up of instruments such as mandolins and guitars. Bamboo is a popular material for the construction of instruments of all types. The rhythmic accompaniment for the famous "Tinikling" dance is produced by two long bamboo poles that are struck together and then struck against the boards on which they rest, making a clicking sound that tells the dancers how to execute their tricky steps. Smaller bamboo sticks are also played, sounding like castanets when they are struck together. Others have split ends that are struck rhythmically on the palm of the hand.

In addition to the instruments made of bamboo, there are such instruments as drums of wood and of bronze; tom-toms of many different sizes; rattles of wood, metal, gourds, or chains; coconut shells used like wood blocks; hardwood sticks struck together like claves.

Sources on Percussion Instruments of the Philippines

Books

Edgerly, Beatrice, *From the Hunter's Bow*. New York: G. P. Putnam's Sons, 1942.

Malm, William P., *Music Cultures of the Pacific, the Near East, and Asia*. Englewood Cliffs, N.J.: Prentice-Hall, Inc., 1967.

Molina, Antonio J., *Philippine Music*. Manila: Antonio J. Molina, 1962.

Romualdo, Norberto, et al., *The Philippine Progressive Music Series, Advanced Course*. Morristown, N.J.: Silver Burdett Company, 1950

Records

Bayanihan Philippine Dance Company. Monitor 322 and 330

Music of the World's Peoples, Vol. 3. Ethnic Folkways, 4506.

Music of the Magindanao in the Philippines, recorded and annotated by Jose Maceda. Ethnic Folkways, FE 4536.

Philippines Tribal Music. Silliman Music Foundation, Silliman Foundation, Dumaguete City, P. I., 5801.

Elementary Music Series Books

Songs from the Philippines with percussion instrument accompaniment: "Tinikling," *Making Music Your Own*, Book 6; "Song of a Loving Mother," *Discovering Music Together*, Book 6; "Leron," *Growing With Music*, Book 3; "Tinikling," *Exploring Music*, Book 5; "Pounding Rice Song," *This Is Music*, Book 4; "Song of a Loving Mother," *Voices of the World*, (*Together We Sing*, Book 6).

RHYTHM INSTRUMENTS IN THE MUSIC OF THE ARAB COUNTRIES

Melody instruments are now, and have been through their long history, popular in the music of the Arab peoples. Rhythm instruments are also important, however. Many kinds of drums are used; there are drums of copper, bronze, gourds, and pottery; there are drums with frames of wood or of baked clay. Hand drums are the most popular. There are large cymbals and finger cymbals, tambourines, and bells. In some areas rattles, clappers, and castanets are used. In addition to all of these, dances and songs are also accompanied by human percussion playing, hand clapping, and stamping. Elementary school boys and girls enjoy the music of the Arab countries and can play typical rhythm instrument accompaniments without much difficulty.

Sources on Rhythm Instruments of the Arab Countries

Books

Bauer, Marion, and Ethel R. Peyser, *Music Through the Ages* (edited and revised by Elizabeth E. Rogers). New York: G. P. Putnam's Sons, 1967.

Malm, William P., *Music Cultures of the Pacific, the Near East, and Asia.* Englewood Cliffs, N.J.: Prentice-Hall, Inc., 1967.

Monsour, Sally, *Folk Songs of the Arab World.* Glendale, Calif.: Bowmar Records, Inc., 1969. Book and sound filmstrip.

Tooze, Ruth, and Beatrice P. Krone. *Literature and Music as Resources for Social Studies.* Englewood Cliffs, N.J.: Prentice-Hall, Inc., 1955.

Records

Folk Instruments of the World. Follett Publishing Company, Album L24.

Music of the Arab People, Morocco, Algeria, Tunisia, Vols. I and II. Esoteric, 2002 and 2003.

Music of the World's Peoples, Vols. 1 and 5. Ethnic Folkways, 4504 and 4508.

Elementary Music Series Books

Songs of the Arab peoples that have rhythm instrument accompaniments: "Tumba," *This Is Music,* Book 6; "Taffta Hindi," *Discovering Music Together,* Book 6; "All Be Brothers, Hallelu," *Growing With Music,* Book 4; "Ala Delona," *Making Music Your Own,* Book 4; "Rocking Camel Caravan," *Music Near and Far* (*Music for Living,* Book 4); "Song of Comrades," *Voices of the World* (*Together We Sing,* Book 6); "Tumba," *Discovering Music Together,* Book 7; "Toomba," *Music for Young Americans,* Book 8.

RHYTHM INSTRUMENTS
IN THE FOLK MUSIC
OF ISRAEL

In some ways, the musical culture of Israel is very old and strongly influenced by geography and by religious and national history; in other ways it is very modern and Western in character. To Western ears, both the folk music and the instruments seem to be closely related to those of the other nations of the Middle East, particularly the Arab nations. At the same time, the music and instruments have a distinctive individuality, perhaps because of their relationship to the pioneer life of many Israelis. It is important for American boys and girls to be acquainted with some of the songs and dances of Israel, and in this connection it is essential to make use of the percussion instruments that are so much a part of the color of the music.

Percussion instruments used with Israeli music include many kinds of drums, large and small, tambourines, and cymbals. The basic rhythm of the music is usually produced by a drum; a very popular type of drum is one made of baked clay and shaped like a jar, wide at one end and narrow at the other, with a drum head over one end. The player holds the instrument under his arm and beats out the rhythm with one hand while also changing the pitch of the sound by manipulating the drum head with his free hand. Clapping and stamping also help to provide a rhythmic accompaniment for many dances. All of this percussive rhythm is combined with instruments such as accordion, recorder, guitar, and mandolin in the Israeli dance orchestras.

Sources on
of Music of Israel and
the Use of Percussion
Instruments

Books

Malm, William P., *Music Cultures of the Pacific, the Near East, and Asia.* Englewood Cliffs, N.J.: Prentice-Hall, Inc., 1967.

Records

Folk Dance in Israel Today. Collectors Guild, CG 638.
Folk Instruments of the World. Follett Publishing Company, Album L24.
(The) Folk Songs and Dances of Israel. Capitol-Angel Records, DT 10490.
Music of the World's Peoples, Vol. 2. Ethnic Folkways, 4505.

Elementary Music Series Books

Songs from Israel with percussion instrument accompaniment: "Boom Dali Da," *Discovering Music Together,* Book 5; "Drawing of the Water," *This Is Music,* Book 5; "Tzena, tzena," *Making Music Your Own,* Book 5; "Toembai," *Making Music (Music for Young Americans,* Book 5); "Song of the Pioneers," *The Magic of Music,* Book 4; "Al Hasela," *Exploring Music,* Book 3; "Dundai," *Music Around the World (Music for Living,* Book 6); "Debka Hora," *Voices of the World (Together We Sing,* Book 6).

MISCELLANEOUS:
PERCUSSION INSTRUMENTS
OF VARIOUS PEOPLES

There are many other kinds of folk and national percussion instruments from important parts of the world that are of interest to boys and girls and that can provide valuable musical and social activities in the elementary school classroom. For example, percussion instruments are used with a great deal of the folk music of the United States and Canada; they are important as a means of adding special national flavor to the music of most countries of Europe; they are used to express national and also tribal individuality in many areas of Africa, Asia, and Australia that are not specifically mentioned here. The voices of percussion instruments are essential to the production of the unique sound present in the music of each particular area. Children in our classrooms will increase their understanding of different ethnic groups and their sensitivity to other cultures through their experiences with a variety of kinds of indigenous music.

Within our own country we have not only the rich heritage of the American Indian music discussed on page 64, but also the music and instruments of many other important groups. Mention was made of the music of Puerto Rico on page 67. Another unique and interesting type of native music is that of Hawaii.

HAWAIIAN MUSIC: THE USE OF NATIVE PERCUSSION INSTRUMENTS

Hawaiian native music in its styles and its instruments shows the influence of both the South Pacific and the West. Stringed instruments of the guitar and ukulele types, together with a variety of percussion instruments, produce a kind of music unlike that of any other part of our country.

Types of Hawaiian Percussion Instruments

Hawaiian native percussion instruments include: drums; the *ipu*, a large, hollowed-out gourd shaped like a jar, played by slapping the sides; the *pu'ili*, a piece of bamboo that is fringed on one end so that it makes a swishing sound when it is struck; the *'ili 'ili*, small flat volcanic rocks that are struck or rubbed together; the *'uli 'uli*, gourd rattles topped with feathers; bamboo poles of varying lengths, that are held vertically, one in each hand, and struck on the ground rhythmically. Clapping and stamping are also used to provide rhythmic accompaniment for dancing. These percussion instruments and their characteristic rhythmic accompaniment are of great interest to boys and girls in the elementary school. Also, if native instruments are not available, highly satisfactory substitutes can be made and used successfully by the children. Suggestions on the use of the ukulele and guitar are given on pages 118 and 123.

Sources on
Hawaiian Music and
Percussion Instruments

Books

Doll, Edna, and Mary Jarman Nelson, *Rhythms Today!* Morristown, N.J.: Silver Burdett Company, 1965.

Kahananui, Dorothy M., *Music of Ancient Hawaii.* Honolulu: University of Hawaii, 1962.

Krone, Beatrice P., and Kurt R. Miller, *Help Yourself to Music* (2nd ed.). Belmont, Calif.: Wadsworth Publishing Company, Inc., 1968.

Malm, William P., *Music Cultures of the Pacific, the Near East, and Asia.* Englewood Cliffs, N.J.: Prentice-Hall, Inc., 1967.

Nye, Robert E., and Vernice T. Nye, *Music in the Elementary School* (3rd ed.). Englewood Cliffs, N.J.: Prentice-Hall, Inc., 1970.

Tooze, Ruth, and Beatrice P. Krone, *Literature and Music as Resources for Social Studies.* Englewood Cliffs, N.J.: Prentice-Hall, Inc., 1955.

Records

Folk Instruments of the World. Follet Publishing Company, Album L24.

Hawaiian Chant, Hula and Music. Ethnic Folkways, 8750.

Souvenirs of Hawaii. Decca, L 5319.

Elementary Music Series Books

Hawaiian songs with percussion instrument accompaniment: "My Boat," *This Is Music,* Book 3; "Hawaiian Stick Game," *Exploring Music,* Book 3; "Alekoki," *Making Music Your Own,* Book 4; "Nani Wale Na Hala," *Making Music Your Own,* Book 5 (also recorded); "Drill Dance," *Making Music Your Own,* Book 6; "My Boat Is Sailing," *Growing With Music,* Book 6; "Heeia," *Discovering Music Together,* Book 3; "Hawaiian Chant," *Studying Music* (*Music for Young Americans,* Book 6).

7

Tuned Bar Instruments
and Keyboard Instruments

The term "tuned bar instruments" as used here refers to melody percussion instruments made up of tuned bars and played with mallets or beaters. The term is used to distinguish these instruments from others in the percussion family, such as those discussed in the section on page 63.

Since many of the classroom activities that use tuned bar instruments and those that use keyboard instruments are similar, and since much of the music used by the two kinds of instruments is generally alike, the two types are considered here together.

TUNED BAR
INSTRUMENTS

Factory-made tuned bar instruments for classroom use are designated by a variety of traditional and trade names, including the following: xylophone, marimba, melody bells, song bells, orchestra bells, glockenspiel, metallophone, step bells, sonant bars, resonator bells, tone bars. Some of these instruments have wooden bars; some have metal bars. Some have resonators beneath the bars and some do not. In some cases the bars are set firmly in a frame; in other cases they are removable; in still other cases the bars are all separate and individual, with no frame. Some instruments are black and white in imitation of the piano keyboard; many have the natural color of the material of which they are made, perhaps polished wood or metal.

Some of these classroom instruments have a range of only one octave. Others have a wide range of many octaves. Some instruments, especially those first used by very small children, include only the diatonic scale. This may be the C scale; again, the bars may be tuned to other scales, for example F or D. Many instruments have bars for all the notes of the chromatic scale. Instruments with a range of several octaves usually have their lowest notes in the neighborhood of Middle C. Sometimes the instruments with a very small range include a scale that ascends from c'' or f'', and therefore the notes they produce are an octave above the normal singing range of the child. A few instruments include the octave below Middle C, and these are especially valuable in the upper grades where voices are deepening.

Instruments selected for school use should produce a sound that is of good quality musically. It is important for boys and girls to use instruments that are accurately tuned and that have a good musical tone. Investment in a few good instruments will be far more profitable than the purchase of many cheap ones, which may be tinny in sound and out of tune with each other and with the musical scale.

Some melody percussion instruments can be made and tuned in the classroom by the teacher and the children. The simplest and probably the most practical to make in the ordinary schoolroom are tuned water glasses and tuned bottles. Suggestions for making them are to be found in *Wake Up and Sing!*, Beatrice Landeck and Elizabeth Crook (New York: Edward B. Marks Corporation, 1969), in *Making Music Your Own*, Books 1 and 2 and in *This Is Music*, Books 1 and 2. (See Appendix, page 129.) In addition to the tuned glasses and bottles, it is possible (though not easy) to make melody percussion instruments by tuning such things as tea cups, clay flower pots, nails and spikes, wooden bars and metal tubes or bars. A great deal of hard work and skill must go into the making of such instruments, however, if they are to have good tone quality and be well-tuned. Suggestions for making a variety of such instruments, both simple and complex, are to be found in *Creative Music in the Home* by Satis Coleman (Valparaiso, Ind.: Lewis E. Myers and Co., 1927).

KEYBOARD
INSTRUMENTS

There are many kinds of keyboard instruments that can be used profitably in classroom music activities. The instrument most frequently found in schools is, of course, the piano. Many elementary schools have classroom pianos that were constructed specifically for school use and are small enough to be moved easily, although they have full-sized keyboards.

Several instruments belonging to the organ family are also useful in teaching the elementary school general music class. The reed organ, because of the quality of its tone, is very well suited to the playing of accompaniments for the light voices of elementary school boys and girls. Some schools have small reed organs that were built for classroom use and are easy for children to play and to move. These little instruments have a keyboard of only a few octaves, but it is adequate for the classroom playing activities of the children. The electric organ is also sometimes used, although it is considerably more complex than the reed organ.

There are also many other kinds of electric instruments in the organ family, some of them with small, accordion-sized keys and others with full-sized keys, some of them large instruments and others small and easily portable. Some are known as chord organs since they have not only a keyboard of a few octaves, but also buttons for producing chords.

In addition to the standard piano, there are various types of keyboard instruments that have electronically produced sound. The tone of these instruments is unique—it is unlike that of either piano or organ. The electronic piano can, under certain circumstances, make a very useful teaching device in the classroom. Some of these instruments have earphone attachments so that a child can practice without disturbing the class; they may also have a monitor system, which permits the teacher to hear any one of several of the instruments being used silently in the classroom. Most of these instruments have keyboards smaller in extent than a standard piano keyboard.

Another instrument related to the keyboard family, and especially to the organ in so far as its sound is concerned, is the *Melodica*. This is a small wind instrument similar in sound to a harmonica, with a miniature keyboard of two octaves or less and keys like those on an accordion. It is easy to play and is particularly valuable as a means of giving children the opportunity to produce music for themselves, whether they play by ear or from notation.

CLASSROOM ACTIVITIES
WITH TUNED BAR
INSTRUMENTS AND
KEYBOARD INSTRUMENTS

Aural Activities
with the Instruments

1. The teacher can enrich the classroom music experiences by playing song melodies and accompaniments on any of these instruments while the class sings.

2. Small children (or those with very limited musical experience) are often confused as to the meaning of terms frequently used in music, such as *high* and *low*. Using one of the tuned bar instruments or a keyboard instrument, the teacher can play such notes as Middle C and c″, the octave above, asking, "Which of these notes is higher?" And then, "Can you sing the high note I am playing? The low note?" When a melody or scale that moves upward or downward in a clearly defined way is played, the suggestion may be, "Move your hands up or down in the direction the music moves." It is helpful to suspend a tuned bar instrument vertically and to play high and low notes as the class watches, listens, and sings, to reinforce the understanding of these concepts.

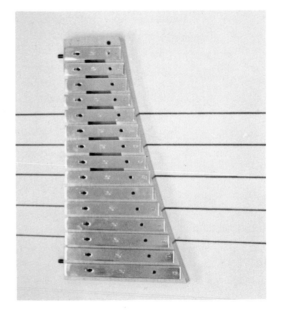

3. The instruments can be used to give experience in hearing and recognizing melodies. Play a familiar song (or a phrase) for recognition. Small children and inexperienced groups sometimes find that a familiar tune sounds strange and new when only the melody is heard without the words. When the song has been identified, play a phrase or two from it and ask: "What words do we sing to this phrase?" Soon they should begin to notice repeated and contrasting phrases, and perhaps to show their recognition of simple song form by making patterns such as ABA or AABA.

4. The above activities are carried on entirely by listening to music that is *heard*. Boys and girls who have had some experience reading notes will also enjoy opening their books to the song they are hearing and finding the exact group of notes played by the teacher or a classmate.

Playing the Instruments in the Classroom

1. *First experiences with tuned bar instruments.* Children want to play these instruments as soon as they see and hear them. Learning how to make a sound on such an instrument, and how to tap the bars so as to produce a clear tone are important early experiences for every interested child. It is also important for boys and girls to get acquainted with the range and dynamics of the instrument, and to learn where to find high and low notes and how to produce sounds that are soft or loud.

2. *First experiences with keyboard instruments.* In much the same way as with the tuned bar instruments, children should be encouraged to get acquainted with the sound of the keyboard instrument, especially the sound of the piano. They need also to discover the range of any available keyboard instrument and the direction in which to move on the keyboard in order to produce high and low pitches.

3. *Playing a simple ostinato part.* For the first actual playing of one of these instruments while the class is singing, the use of a simple ostinato part is recommended. This is a part made up of only a small group of notes, sometimes only one or two, which are repeated over and over as an accompaniment to a familiar song being sung. This type of part is quickly learned and allows a child to relax and feel confident as he repeats the same sequence of notes many times while the class sings, whereas if he attempts to play all the notes in the melody, he must first acquire considerable skill. Playing a simple ostinato accompaniment is an activity of interest and value to all age levels. It is possible for small children, even at the kindergarten

level, to carry on many such activities successfully. Older boys and girls enjoy and profit from playing an ostinato part; they improve their knowledge of music through repeated use of a few notes; they also develop a basic skill in hearing and using a simple harmony part. Here are some suggestions for the use of an ostinato part with a familiar song.

ROUND AND ROUND AND ROUND

Words and Music by Vic Marantz

Round and round and round,   Round and round and round, At the ending of the song I   found That the mu-sic kept on go-ing round.

From *Growing With Music*, Book 5, p. 178. © 1966 by Prentice-Hall, Inc.

a. While the class sings, one child plays Middle C over and over rhythmically throughout the song on a tuned bar or keyboard instrument. This requires some rhythmic skill as well as the ability to produce the note on the instrument; the player must be able to respond to the recurring rhythmic beat in the music. Other simple ostinati, such as are given below, can be played as the children's skill increases. This playing is done entirely by rote in most classes, although in case of tuned bar instruments, if there are letter names on the bars, some children at every grade level soon recognize that the notes they are playing over and over again have the letter names of C, F, or A. Before long they develop a sure sense of the distance between the various notes used. If the tuned bars are suspended vertically over a chalkboard, a staff in line with the notes of the bars will make this relationship obvious, even without special attention.

b. Often the children will sing the simple ostinato as they play it, sometimes with a neutral syllable like "la," and sometimes with appropriate words, such as "Round and round and," etc., for pattern 2 above or "Sing, sing" for 3. When a keyboard instrument or an instrument with fixed bars is used, it will help unskilled players if the notes to be played are marked so that they are easily found. If the instruments have removable bars, it is possible at first in playing the patterns above to remove all the bars not being used, leaving only those that are to be played as is shown in the picture that follows. Since these bars are firmly anchored, the relative distance between the notes is clearly seen and the children soon begin to sense the extent of an octave. If the disconnected resonator bars are used, the separate bars can each be played by a different child.

c. Most classes of small children will sing this song in unison, but experienced singers can use it as a round, each group of singers in the round having one or more ostinato players accompanying it.

4. *Playing by ear.* The teacher plays one or two notes, using a recorder flute or a tuned bar instrument. One child at a time tries to find, on

his instrument, the note he heard and play it. Sometimes the teacher or a child will sing a question, while playing the notes for it on the bars. Another child answers, trying to play the same notes on his instrument, and also to sing them. This is an excellent way to help a child learn to sing in tune, since he can reinforce his voice by playing the notes as he sings. Small groups of notes and classroom conversations can be created for such activities. Here are some examples.

A keyboard instrument can be used in the same way as the tuned bar instrument, with each child listening to the notes the teacher plays or sings and then trying to find them at the keyboard.

5. *Playing song accompaniments: pentatonic.* Interesting ostinato and harmony parts can be played as accompaniments to many of the songs the children sing. Some of these are very easy, but others require considerable skill and coordination. Except for gifted children, therefore, this type of activity is usually most successful in classes beyond the primary level. Most of these accompaniments will be learned by rote, although children who have begun to use the musical score will enjoy seeing the notation for the parts they are playing.

Songs based on the pentatonic scale (1-2-3-5-6) are most easily adaptable to varied ostinato accompaniments, and there are many of these songs in every elementary school series music book. When children have had experience playing one or two note ostinati, as suggested above, they will want to increase their musical vocabulary by including more extensive patterns. The first orchestrations used in this way should be very easy and should use only a few instruments.

Here is a song based on the pentatonic scale, and with it are some ostinato patterns such as may be played by the tuned bar or keyboard instruments for accompaniment.

BIRD'S COURTING SONG

New England Folk Song

Gaily

Hi! said the black - bird, sit - ting on a chair,

Once I court - ed a la - dy fair, She proved fick-le and

Turned her back, And ev - er since then I've dressed in black.

Refrain

Tow - dy, ow - dy, did- dle - o - dum,

Tow - dy, ow - dy, did-dle-o - day; Tow-dy, ow - dy,

did - dle- o - dum, Tow -dy, ow - dy, did-dle -o - day.

From *Growing With Music*, Book 5, p. 180. © 1966 by Prentice-Hall, Inc.

Suggested classroom activities:

a. If instruments with removable bars are used, remove all the bars
   except those in the pentatonic scale on G (G, A, B, D, E) or all
   bars not needed for the ostinato being played on the instrument,
   leaving G, A, D, E. If the bars cannot be removed, mark these

notes clearly so they will be easy to identify. This can also be done with notes on a piano keyboard. The instruments will look approximately like those in the illustrations that follow.

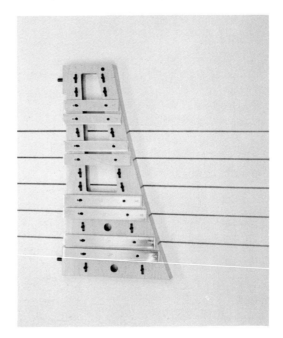

b. Have one child play pattern No. 1 (D, E, G, A) several times for the class to hear. Then, as the class sings the song, have No. 1 played as an accompaniment. This will allow the children to hear the contrapuntal effect of the one instrument part as it is played with the melody. One of the greatest values of this type of activity is the musicianship and keenness of hearing it can develop, and these develop only when it is possible to hear clearly and to discriminate between different musical sounds. Too many different sounds heard at first will cause confusion. Several children can take turns playing this same accompaniment pattern.

c. Later another child plays pattern No. 2 for the class to hear. Use it alone as an accompaniment for the song so that it can be clearly heard. Have 1 and 2 played together as a duet for the class to hear. Then, as the class sings the song, the *two* patterns accompany it.

d. Add pattern No. 3 in the same way, first allowing the player an opportunity to practice it. When all three patterns have been used with the song, one or more of them can be selected to play as an introduction. If a keyboard instrument is being used, unless more than one piano is available, pattern 3 can be omitted; otherwise patterns 1 and 3 will overlap. Or pattern 3 can be played softly in a higher octave.

e. If several kinds of tuned bar instruments are available, the orchestration produced will have variety and uniqueness of sound. For example, pattern No. 1 could be played by the alto xylophone, 2 by the alto glockenspiel, and 3 by the soprano glockenspiel; this would produce variety in both pitch and type of sound. It will add greatly to the musical value of such activities as they take place with different kinds of songs, to use instruments of different pitches, high and low, and of different types of construction, wood, metal, and resonator and non-resonator. The xylophones, marimbas, metallophones and glockenspiels with removable bars are the most flexible instruments for developing these fundamental skills, but instruments with fixed bars can also be used. Since only a few children at a time play on most song accompaniments, a few instruments will be sufficient for any one song, but it is valuable to have an assortment of instruments of different types from which to choose. With some songs only one instrument may be sufficient to provide an accompaniment; sometimes a light, delicate descant or ostinato is enough and more will ruin the effect and confuse the ear.

6. *The pentatonic on the black keys.* Another easy way to experiment with the pentatonic scale is to use the black keys on the piano or the chromatic bars on the tuned bells. These notes make up a complete pentatonic scale based on G♭. Any pentatonic melody can be played on them and an accompaniment for it can be created by using any combination of one or more of these black key notes and playing them to fit the rhythm of the song. For example, the song given on page 93, "Bird's Courting Song," can be played on the black keys or the chromatic bars by starting G♭, E♭, etc. It is possible to play on the black keys or chromatic bars the same melody and the same ostinato patterns as were given above using G, A, B, D, E, except that the notes will now be G♭, A♭, B♭ D♭, and E♭.

7. *Creating song accompaniments: pentatonic.* Ostinato patterns suitable for use with familiar songs can be created by the boys and girls. If the song is based on the pentatonic scale, any of the notes of that scale can be played to accompany the melody without producing an unpleasant dissonance. For example, an ostinato accompaniment might be created for the familiar song, "Ol' Texas."

OL' TEXAS

If instruments with removable bars are available, remove all the bars except those for the notes of the pentatonic scale that begins on F: F, G, A, C, D. If the bars cannot be removed, or if a keyboard instrument is used, mark these same notes clearly at first, so that they will be easy to identify.

a. Let the children experiment with the sound of the instruments by playing the notes of this five-tone scale softly and rhythmically up and down the full range of the instrument while the song is being sung. The exact notes that would be played in this way will depend on the type and range of the instruments, but they may be something like those given on the lower staff of "Ol' Texas."

The children should next experiment with creating simple patterns, each of which uses just a few of the notes in this scale; repeat a pattern continuously as an accompaniment to the song, fitting it to the song rhythm. A steady, simple pattern will usually be more effective than a complex or elaborate one. Effective ostinato patterns for songs in the pentatonic often use the following notes of the scale: do, re, sol, and la (1, 2, 5, 6), sometimes playing two of these notes simultaneously, and other times in a pattern that uses two or three or more notes in a repeated sequence: 1, 2, 1, 2, or 1, 5, 6, 5, 1, etc. Have the class listen to the ostinato patterns created by individual children and choose those they think fit the music best. If several are selected, the effect will be more musical when they are different from each other in pitch and speed. One can be slow and sustained, another more active; one high, another low; one can move in an upward, another in a downward direction. Children who have learned to read notes often enjoy writing the notation of the ostinato parts they create.

8. *Playing the melody.* Playing the entire melody of a song requires greater skill than that needed to play an easy repeated ostinato accompaniment. Following are some suggestions for developing this skill.

a. Children who have had previous experience playing simple, repeated accompaniments to songs, such as those outlined above, will already have developed the skill needed to play simple song melodies. Previous experience using the musical score and an understanding of the rhythmic and melodic notation is necessary if boys and girls are to succeed in playing songs from their books. They may, however, play some of their familiar songs by ear, without the use of notes.

b. In the limited time available in the general classroom, children can successfully master the skill of playing a melody that the class is singing if the melody is not too complex and if they are allowed to build their skill gradually, using familiar songs and playing only part of the notes at first, perhaps the first note in each phrase or measure. This type of experience gives a child an opportunity to play his few notes and at the same time adjust his playing to the rhythmic beat of the music and the speed of the singing. Most of the problems children have in playing a melody while the class sings it are the problems of adjusting to the speed or the rhythm of the music. For example, in the song below, if the instruments play only the first three notes in each phrase, while the class sings the entire song, the players will have time enough to get themselves ready, musically and physically, to play each time.

A CRADLE HYMN

Isaac Watts
Johann Sebastian Bach

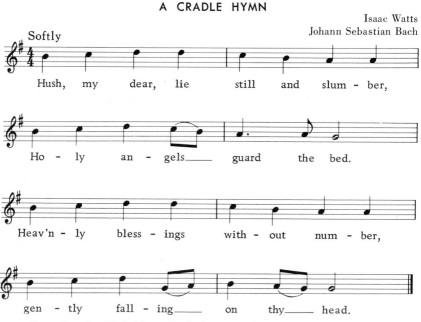

From *Growing With Music*, Book 4, p. 130. © 1966 by Prentice-Hall, Inc.

c. In the song "Intry Mintry," if the boys and girls start by playing only the first note in each measure, they will have only two notes to think about, E and G, and they will soon learn to keep pace with the speed of the singing. Before long they will also be playing other groups of notes, such as the last measure of each phrase; soon the entire song will be possible.

INTRY MINTRY

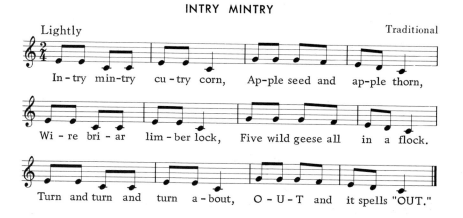

In - try min-try   cu - try corn,   Ap-ple seed and   ap-ple thorn,

Wi - re bri - ar   lim - ber lock,   Five wild geese all   in   a   flock.

Turn   and turn   and   turn   a - bout,   O - U - T   and   it spells "OUT."

d. Songs chosen for the first attempts at playing should contain familiar rhythms and notes, but soon the challenge of playing the melody will lead many children to acquire a great deal more knowledge about the musical score than they would ordinarily have. With good instruments and an opportunity to practice on them, they learn to use such musical ideas as chromatics, unfamiliar scale patterns and contemporary music that is based upon a tone row.

e. When tuned bar instruments are used, sometimes instead of having the voices sing the melody while ostinato or harmony parts accompany it, a classroom orchestra can be developed, with some instruments playing the melody, while others play the counterpoint or harmony of the accompaniment.

9. *Playing song accompaniments: chord roots.* Simple harmony parts are more appropriate for many songs than a repeated ostinato. Skill in playing, singing and creating such parts can be developed in much the same way as was suggested for the use of the ostinato. A song that normally needs only one or two or at most three chords to complete its basic harmonization is best for the first experience of this kind. Here is an example of a suitable song for this type of activity.

SING TOGETHER

From *Growing With Music*, Book 5, p. 10. © 1966 by Prentice-Hall, Inc.

Suggested classroom activities with songs such as the above:

a. The first chording activities are usually taught by rote. Play only the root of the chord. If the autoharp chord symbols are given with the song, as is the case with "Sing Together," they will indicate the notes to be played: G, G, G, G, G, D, G, etc.

b. As the song is being sung, play the notes of the chord root as an accompaniment lightly and rhythmically on tuned bars or a keyboard instrument. In some songs this will mean playing on the accented beats only; in other songs it will mean playing on each beat. This will depend on the tempo of the song and the number of chord changes desirable in harmonizing it.

c. Encourage the children to sing the notes as they play them, using a neutral syllable like "la, la," or singing the letter names or syllables or numbers. Sometimes words suitable for the song can be used. In the song above, the words might be, "Sing, sing."

d. It is important to allow every interested child the opportunity to try playing this type of instrumental part.

e. If a keyboard instrument is being used, encourage the children to play the chord root tones in various octaves. The notes in the octave below Middle C are especially effective for accompanying a song on the piano or on a tuned bar instrument which includes bars in the low range. This experience is helpful to older boys whose voices are deepening; as they play the few notes which are used in this kind of accompaniment, they will often begin to match these pitches with their own singing voices.

f. The small tympani mentioned under the section on the Orff instruments, page 52, can also be used for these activities. There are usually three of these instruments and they can be tuned to play the chord roots to accompany songs.

g. As the children's skill increases, songs with more chord changes, in both major and minor modes can be used in the same way. Many of the songs the class sings can be accompanied with these chord root notes, and before long the children will develop the ability to recognize by ear the correct notes to be played.

10. *Playing chords.* Intermediate or upper grade boys and girls who have had some of the experiences suggested above will enjoy learning to play not just the chord roots, but the entire chords, at the piano. Even children who are taking piano lessons may not have been taught how to chord, so this is usually an activity of great interest to the entire class.

a. The first song used in this way can well be a familiar round that can be harmonized with the use of only one chord. For example, if "Row, Row, Row Your Boat" is sung in key of C, a chording accompaniment like the following can be played:

 etc.

Give the children the opportunity to play this, sometimes with the right hand, sometimes using the left hand, while the class sings the song. It is not easy for a beginner to play three notes simultaneously at first, but most children, given the opportunity to learn, will find ways to practice playing chords until they are able to do it smoothly. When this can be done easily, change to a new chord in the next to the last measure ("Life is but a dream").

b. Next choose another song requiring a second chord, which can be played in "close" position so that the hand does not have to skip around the keyboard. For example, the following song could be chorded as shown.

WHISTLE, MARY, WHISTLE

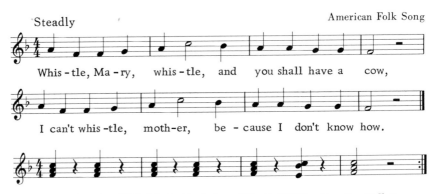

From *Growing With Music*, Book 4, p. 101. © 1966 by Prentice-Hall, Inc.

These chords can be played with either the right hand or the left hand. They will usually be learned by rote, but if notation is used, it can be in the bass clef as well as in the treble clef.

c. Before long, some boys and girls will be ready to add other chords and to vary a simple accompaniment such as the one above by using broken chords.

d. This much introduction to chording will lead many children to the playing of more complex chording accompaniments requiring wider movement of the hand. At first, two children can work together, one playing the melody and the other the chords. Eventually some individuals will be using both hands to play the melody with the chordal accompaniment.

e. Children with special interest and ability will frequently extend their knowledge to include understanding of such musical concepts as: cadence, inversion, and chord numbering or lettering of the following types, I, IV, V^7, vi; C, G^7, Dm.

11. *Playing part songs.* Students in classes where part songs are being sung can profit from learning to play two- or three-part songs on the instruments. Songs with sustained harmonies are especially suitable for such activity. Children have a practical grasp of a harmony part in a song they are singing, and particularly of a lower part or

an inner voice, when they have played one or more parts on an instrument, in ensemble with other instruments. They sense the relationship of each part to the whole, instead of attempting to use one part as an independent unit. This kind of activity is an excellent means of developing ability to sustain a part with the voice.

**Sources on
Playing Tuned Bar
and Keyboard Instruments
in the Classroom***

Books

Garretson, Robert L., *Music in Childhood Education*. New York: Appleton-Century-Crofts, 1966.

Gary, Charles L., ed., *The Study of Music in the Elementary School*. Washington, D.C.: Music Educators National Conference, 1967.

Landeck, Beatrice and Elizabeth Crook, *Wake Up and Sing!* New York: Edward B. Marks Music Corporation, 1969.

Leach, John R., *Functional Piano for the Teacher*. Englewood Cliffs, N.J.: Prentice-Hall, Inc., 1968.

Nelson, Mary Jarman, and Gladys Tipton, *Music for Early Childhood*. Morristown, N.J.: Silver Burdett Company, 1952.

Nye, Robert E., and Vernice T. Nye, *Exploring Music with Children*, Belmont, Calif.: Wadsworth Publishing Company, Inc., 1966.

————, *Music in the Elementary School* (3rd ed.). Englewood Cliffs, N.J.: Prentice-Hall, Inc., 1970.

Rainbow, Bernarr, ed., *Handbook for Music Teachers*, Book I. London: Novello and Co., Ltd., 1964.

Rinderer, Leo, *Music Education*. English translation by Edmund A. Cykler and John R. Keith. Park Ridge, Ill.: Neil A. Kjos Music Company, Publisher, 1961.

Runkle, Aleta, and Mary LeBow Eriksen, *Music for Today's Boys and Girls*. Boston: Allyn & Bacon, Inc., 1966.

Slind, Lloyd, and D. Evan Davis, *Bringing Music to Children*. New York: Harper & Row, Publishers, 1964.

Swanson, Bessie R., *Music in the Education of Children* (3rd ed.). Belmont, Calif.: Wadsworth Publishing Company, Inc., 1969.

White, Florence, and Kazuo Akiyama, *Children's Songs from Japan*. New York: Edward B. Marks Music Corp., 1960.

---

* Also see page 127 for list of music for classroom ensembles.

Elementary Music Series Books

(There is a great wealth of song material available for classroom tuned bar and keyboard instrument activity at various grade levels in every current music series. These materials include the use of the instruments in connection with such experiences as learning to sing, getting acquainted with music notation, and playing descants, ostinati, and harmony parts. Only a few examples can be listed here.)

1. *Pentatonic ostinato parts:* "Hush, My Baby," *This Is Music,* Book 2; "Creating Music," *Growing With Music,* Book 5; "Rock Island Line" (verse), *Growing With Music,* Book 5; "Down Came a Lady," *This Is Music,* Book 4; "Making Up Music," *Growing With Music,* Book 3; "The Riddle Song," *Exploring Music,* Book 4; "A Good Day in Japan," *Exploring Music,* Book 4; "Gold and Silver Bells," *The Magic of Music,* Book 3; "Mother Horse," *Discovering Music Together,* Teacher's Edition, Book 1; "Song of Bluebells," *Discovering Music Together,* Book 6; "Tideo," *Basic Goals in Music,* Book 5.

2. *Miscellaneous types of descants and ostinati for instruments:* "The Dairy Maids," *Growing With Music,* Book 4; "Ah, Poor Bird," *Growing With Music,* Books 2 and 6; "Oranges and Lemons," *Growing With Music,* Book 3; "Skating," *This Is Music,* Book 3; "Patsy," *This Is Music,* Book 4; "Rainy Day," *Understanding Music (Music for Young Americans,* Book 4); "Vesper Hymn," *Exploring Music,* Book 3; "Fiesta Day," *The Magic of Music,* Books 3 and 4; "Come Rowing with Me," *Discovering Music Together,* Book 3; "Adieu To My Comrades," *Making Music Your Own,* Book 5; "See-Saw, Margery Daw," *Music 'Round the Clock (Together We Sing,* Book 1); "The Man on the Flying Trapeze," *Music 'Round the Town (Together We Sing,* Book 2); "Coffee Grows," *Basic Goals in Music,* Book 2.

3. *Using the piano keyboard:* "Beautiful Apples," *Discovering Music Together,* Book 2; "Old Brass Wagon," *Discovering Music Together,* Book 4; "After School," *Exploring Music,* Book 2; "Taffy," *Exploring Music (Music for Young Americans,* Book 3); "The Bells," *Growing With Music,* Book 3; "At the Piano," *This Is Music,* Book 3; "Let's Explore the Piano," *This Is Music,* Book 2; "Moonlight," *The Magic of Music,* Book 2; "Old Polina," *Making Music Your Own,* Book 5; "The Campbells Are Coming," *This Is Music,* Book 5; "We're on the Upward Trail," *Basic Goals in Music,* Book 4; "Introduction to the Piano," *Basic Goals in Music,* Book 3.

4. *Pentatonic on the black keys:* "Sheep Are Grazing," *Making Music Your Own,* Book 4; "Trot, Pony, Trot," *Discovering Music Together,* Book 3; "Hato Popo," *Making Music Your Own,* Book 3; "After School," *Exploring Music,* Book 2; "Trot, Pony Trot," *Exploring Music,* Book 1; "Raindrops," *Meeting Music (Music for Young Americans,* Book 1); "Rain," *This Is Music,* Book 1; "Good-by," *The Magic of Music,* Book 4; "Lotus Blossoms," *Discovering Music Together,* Book 7; "Land of the Silver Birch," *Basic Goals in Music,* Book 4.

5. *Chord roots and piano chording:* "Jig Along Home," *Growing With Music,* Book 4; "Animal Song," *Growing With Music,* Book 4; "Springfield Mountain," *This Is Music,* Book 5; "Chopsticks," *Growing With Music,* Book 5; "Good-Night, Ladies," *Understanding Music (Music for Young Americans,* Book 4); "Love Somebody," *Making Music (Music for Young Americans,* Book

5); "Streets of Laredo," *Exploring Music,* Book 6; "The Shanty Boys in the Pine," *Exploring Music,* Book 4; "Getting Acquainted with Chords," *The Magic of Music,* Book 4; "The Deaf Woman's Courtship," *The Magic of Music,* Book 4; "Down the River," *Discovering Music Together,* Book 4; "I Have Lost the *Do,*" *Making Music Your Own,* Book 4; "Holla-hi, Holla-ho!" *The Magic of Music,* Book 5; "Un Cerf Dans Sa Grande Maison," *Basic Goals in Music,* Book 5; "Mistress Shady," *This Is Music,* Book 7; "Paper of Pins," *Music for Young Americans,* Book 7; "My Hat It Has Three Corners" and "My Goose," *Basic Goals in Music,* Book 4; "Clementine," *Music in Our Country (Music for Living,* Book 5).

6. *Playing a melody:* "Kuma San," *Discovering Music Together,* Book 3; "Cascabel," *Making Music Your Own,* Book 3; "Ding Dong Bell," *Exploring Music,* Book 1; "It's Raining," *Exploring Music,* Book 1; "Bell Music," *Discovering Music (Music for Young Americans,* Book 2); "Walking Song," *Growing With Music,* Book 3; "Twinkle, Twinkle, Little Star," *This Is Music,* Book 2; "My Little Train," *The Magic of Music,* Primer and Book 1; "See the Little Ducklings," *The Magic of Music,* Book 2; "French Cradle Song," *The Magic of Music,* Book 3; "Abreme la puerta, Nina," *Making Music Your Own,* Book 2.

7. *Playing part songs:* "Count the Stars," *Growing With Music,* Book 5; "The Luau," *Growing With Music,* Book 5; "On Top of Old Smoky," *This Is Music,* Book 6; "Chopsticks," *Studying Music (Music for Young Americans,* Book 6); "It's Quiet on the Moon," *Exploring Music,* Book 4; "Kum Ba Yah," *The Magic of Music,* Book 4; "Saturday Night," *Discovering Music Together,* Book 5; "Beautiful Hawaii," *Making Music Your Own,* Book 4; "Stars of the Heavens," *Making Music Your Own,* Book 5.

8

Small Wind Instruments in the Classroom: Recorders and Other Instruments of the Flute Family

Many small instruments of the flute family are valuable and easily available for use in the general classroom music activities. Some of these instruments are constructed so as to be more consistently and reliably in tune than others. Most of them, however, if used with care and musical discrimination can provide the means for broad and interesting musical learnings.

Types of Instruments

1. Instruments made of plastic, with trade names such as: tonette, song flute, flutophone.
2. Instruments made of metal, with names such as: melody flute and fife.
3. Instruments of wood, such as the recorder. (Good recorders made of plastic are also available.)

Preliminary Planning for the Use of Small Winds in the Classroom

1. In order to learn to play one of these small wind instruments, a child must have fingers long enough to reach the holes to be covered. Also,

many children find it easier to play such an instrument if they have their permanent front teeth. It is probably for these reasons, and also because most classes learn to associate the notes they play on the instruments with the visual representation of the same notes on a staff, that most of the songbooks in the elementary school music series include this type of activity for the first time for children who are eight or nine years old. This does not mean, however, that younger children cannot successfully play the small winds if the children are ready for them.

2. It is possible to have everyone in a class playing one of these instruments, but it is often more feasible to have a group made up of those who have special interest in the activity and who are willing to practice to acquire the necessary skill for playing.

3. Most of these instruments are in the key of C, but some are in other keys. It should be self-evident that all instruments used for unison playing in a beginning class must be in the same key, *and in tune with one another.*

4. There are good instructional materials for beginning classes available for each of these types of instruments.· In addition, many of the elementary school music series books include lesson outlines and music for such instruments.

5. In this type of class, as in any type of instrumental class, there must be a plan of activity that is clearly understood by both teacher and students. All children want to blow their flutes as soon as they have them in their hands. Every child will have a more enjoyable experience and will make more satisfactory progress if rules are set up and obeyed. The class period set aside for playing these instruments can be divided into short periods for learning new material—notes, fingering, music theory, playing skills, and so on. Other short periods will be devoted to group playing (sometimes interspersed with group singing) of the notes or music being studied; to individual playing of notes, measures, or passages. Then there can be short periods for general practice, when everyone tries out the new fingering or melodies. An organized plan for the use of the time available for this activity will result in more rapid progress and increased opportunities for every child·in the group.

Learning to
Play the Small Winds

1. Children must learn first of all to blow the instrument correctly. Since the techniques of playing the different instruments vary somewhat, it is suggested that the instructions for each instrument be carefully followed. Boys and girls must learn at once not to over-

blow, or blow too hard. They must also learn to articulate each note, using the tongue lightly as if to say, "Too, too."

2. Learning to play and to sustain just one or two notes correctly is usually better at first than to attempt to learn the entire scale. The first notes to be learned and the fingerings for them will vary according to the specific instrument. Usually the first notes played will be near the middle of the range of the instrument; notes at the extremes, either high or low, are difficult for beginners to play.

3. It is possible to develop a certain amount of skill on these instruments when playing entirely by ear, learning by rote. Most children, however, will readily learn to associate the notes they are playing with the staff notation for them. It is suggested that the notation for the notes they are learning be kept before the class constantly on chalkboard or felt board or in books.

4. Whenever possible, correlate the experience of playing the small wind instruments with classroom singing activities. The suggestions given below the next song illustrate some of the ways of alternating singing and playing in order to allow the teacher to give attention to all individuals in the group.

HA! HA! HA!

From *Growing With Music*, Book 4, p. 90. © 1966 by Prentice-Hall, Inc.

a. It is assumed that the children have previously learned to play the four notes in this song on their instruments.

b. The children play the song; they sing the song. Then the class is divided into two sections, one of which sings while the other plays. Alternate the parts.

c. Individuals sing and play together. This encourages the children to listen, to watch the notes, and to increase their skill in singing and playing from notation. As new fingerings are learned, new notes are placed on the staff and the related singing pitches are also learned. The rhythmic as well as the melodic notation must receive attention.

5. Because of the limited range of some of these instruments, not all songs can be played on them. Children can learn a great deal about their instruments and about music notation by learning to choose which songs they can play.

6. The experience of playing these instruments can furnish an excellent basis for understanding simple harmony. Many of the suggestions given in Chapter 7 for playing descants, ostinati, and simple harmony parts on tuned-bar instruments and keyboard instruments can also be used in playing small wind instruments. Simple descants for small wind instruments are included in many of the elementary school music books. Here are some additional suggestions:

   a. Boys and girls who are beginning to sing part songs will enjoy learning to play these songs as duets or trios on their flutes.

   b. A familiar round can provide a good introduction to such activity. First play it in unison; then divide the group into two sections and play it as a round. The use of a round such as "Are You Sleeping?" in this way can help the children to develop a sure feeling for the harmony produced in singing it.

7. When songs are too fast or too complex to be played on small winds, introductions or postludes can be arranged and played.

SPECIAL CLASSROOM ACTIVITIES FOR THE RECORDER

Almost any of the activities suggested in the preceding section are suitable for use with the recorder. In addition, it should also be remembered that the recorder is a legitimate musical instrument and not one that has been constructed for limited special uses by inexperienced players. There is an important and extensive literature of recorder music. Boys and girls who have learned to play the soprano recorder can, as their hands reach the required size, learn to play other recorders—alto, tenor, and bass. (In English recorder music, the instruments are divided into groups with these names: descant, treble, tenor, and bass.) Because of the musical quality of the recorder tone and the technical flexibility of the instruments, recorders can provide lasting satisfaction for players of all ages in amateur school ensembles and in family and community groups.

The recorder can also serve as a source of varied creative activities in the classroom. In many European countries, both classroom teachers and music teachers use the recorder continually in classroom music. For example:

1. The teacher plays part of a familiar song on the recorder. The children sing the remainder of the song.
2. As the teacher plays the instrument, the children show with their hands the upward and downward movement of the music.
3. The teacher plays the recorder and the children move to the rhythm of the music.
4. When the children are playing tuned bar or keyboard instruments, the teacher plays a phrase of a familiar song on the recorder while the class listens. The children first find the beginning note of the phrase on their instruments; then they pick out the entire phrase by ear. This can also be done with groups of children who are learning to play the recorder.
5. The teacher plays a phrase; a child plays (or sings) an answering phrase he has created.

**Sources on
Playing Small
Wind Instruments
in the Classroom***

Books

Garretson, Robert L., *Music in Childhood Education.* New York: Appleton-Century-Crofts, 1966.

Hunt, E., *The Recorder and Its Music.* New York: W. W. Norton & Company, Inc., 1963.

Nye, Robert E., and Vernice T. Nye, *Music in the Elementary School* (3rd ed.). Englewood Cliffs, N.J.: Prentice-Hall, Inc., 1970.

Rigby, F. F., *Playing the Recorders.* New York: St. Martin's Press, Inc., 1959.

Slind, Lloyd H., and D. Evan Davis, *Bringing Music to Children.* New York: Harper & Row, Publishers, 1964.

Swanson, Bessie R., *Music in the Education of Children* (3rd ed.). Belmont, Calif.: Wadsworth Publishing Company, Inc., 1969.

* Also see page 127 for listing of music for classroom ensembles.

Special Instructional Materials for Small Winds

Bamberger, Gertrud, *Teaching the Recorder to Children.* Far Rockaway, N.Y.: Carl Van Roy Co., Inc., 1962.

Barr, Lawrence, Elizabeth Blair, and Walter Ehret, *You and Music.* Englewood Cliffs, N.J.: Prentice-Hall, Inc., 1959.

Beckman, Frederick, *Classroom Method for Melody Flute.* Laurel, Md.: Melody Flute Co., 1952.

Bradford, Margaret, and Elizabeth Parker, *How to Play the Recorder (Soprano).* New York: G. Schirmer, Inc., 1938.

Buchtel, Forrest L., *Melody Fun Method for the Tonette.* Elmhurst, Ill.: Lyons Band Instrument Co., 1938.

Dinn, Freda, *The Recorder in School.* London: Schott, Pub. (USA: Associated Music Publishers, Inc.), 1965.

Dolmetsch, Carl, *Start My Way.* Bryn Mawr, Penna.: Theodore Presser Company, 1962.

Earle, Frederick. *Music-Time for Flutophone and Other Pre-Band Instruments.* Cleveland: Grossman Co., 1961.

Golding, Sally, and Lucille Landers, *Melody Makers.* Far Rockaway, N.Y.: Carl Van Roy Co., 1962.

Hansen, Rae, *From Rote to Note.* New York: Edward B. Marks Music Corp. n.d.

Hofstad, Mildred, *Very First Favorites for the Soprano Recorder.* New York: G. Schirmer, Inc., 1959.

Katz, Erich, *Recorder Playing.* Far Rockaway, N.Y.: Carl Van Roy Co., 1958.

Kulbach, Johanna, *Tunes for Children.* Far Rockaway, N.Y.: Carl Van Roy Co., 1959.

Modern Musical Fun (for Singing and Playing with the Tonette). Elmhurst, Ill.: Lyons Band Instrument Co., 1967.

Moore, E. C., *Classroom Instructor for the Recorder.* New York: Carl Fischer, Inc., 1964.

———, *Classroom Instructor for the Tonette.* New York: Carl Fischer, Inc., 1964.

Schoch, Rudolf, and Gertrud Bamberger, *To Music with the Soprano Recorder, I and II.* Locarno: Edizioni Pegasus (USA: C. F. Peters Corp., New York), 1964.

Van Pelt, Merrill B. and J. Leon Ruddick, *The Flutophone Classroom Method.* Cleveland: Grossman Company, 1947.

Wachtell, Eva H., *Musical Moments with the Recorder.* New York: G. Schirmer, Inc., 1944.

Weiss, William M., *The Soprano Recorder.* New York: Boosey & Hawkes, 1965.

White, Florence, and Ann Bergman, *Playing the Recorder*. New York: Edward B. Marks Music Corp., 1955.

Woelflen, Leslie E., *Classroom Melody Instruments, a Programed Text*. Glenview, Ill.: Scott, Foresman & Co., 1967. (For flutophone, song flute, tonette, and recorder.)

Elementary Music Series Books

Instructional materials and music for small winds: "Music for Small Winds," *Discovering Music Together*, Book 4; "Flutes," *Understanding Music (Music for Young Americans*, Book 4); "With Small Winds and Autoharp," *This Is Music*, Book 3; "Listen While My Flute Is Playing," *This Is Music*, Book 4; "The Donkey," *Making Music Your Own*, Book 3; "The Careless Shepherd," *Making Music Your Own*, Book 4; "Pat-a-pan," *Growing With Music*, Book 5; "Cashua," *The Magic of Music*, Book 4; "Birds of a Feather," *The Magic of Music*, Book 6; "Playing the Recorder," *Basic Goals in Music*, Book 4; "Skip to My Lou," *Basic Goals in Music*, Book 6; "Cotton-Eyed Joe," *Voices of America (Together We Sing*, Book 5).

9

Stringed Instruments in the General Classroom

Several kinds of stringed instruments are useful for classroom music activities. These include three types: instruments that are made especially for classroom use by children, such as the autoharp, the gamba, the psaltery; instruments used for informal classroom music activities, such as the ukulele, the guitar, and the mandolin; standard stringed instruments that can sometimes be used as learning vehicles for an entire class, such as the cello and the string bass. Some of these instruments are used by children to play melodies by ear or from notation, original or from their music books. Other instruments are used for providing a chordal accompaniment for class singing or for solo or small group performances. Sometimes stringed instruments are used to provide a simple bass accompaniment for songs, usually playing the root of the chord as was suggested in the section on the use of tuned bar and keyboard instruments, page 99.

THE AUTOHARP

The autoharp is an old fashioned zither-like instrument, which has recently come again into popularity. It provides an easy, lazy man's way of playing chords. It is used by folk singers, is frequently seen on TV, and is an exceedingly valuable instrument in the classroom.

Autoharps are available in several sizes, the most common for classroom use being the 12-bar, although 15-bar and 5-bar instruments are also used. Most current school music books include autoharp chords for many songs. These are usually indicated by the chord letter names (C, F, G⁷, etc.), but sometimes the chord numerals are used (I, IV, V⁷, etc.).

Activities for
Classroom Use
of the Autoharp

1. Small children love to have the teacher accompany their songs on the autoharp. Often, before their fingers are strong enough to hold down the chord bars, they enjoy strumming the strings, while the teacher presses the bars.

2. Playing the autoharp requires the ability to strum the strings rhythmically and to press the correct bars at the correct times for the necessary chord changes. Familiar songs that have a smooth rhythmic swing are best for the first playing experiences. Also, choose a song that requires only one or two chords. Here is an example.

I'M GONNA SING

From *Growing With Music*, Book 4, p. 1. © 1966 by Prentice-Hall, Inc.

While the class sings, the teacher plays the autoharp accompaniment, playing the chords where indicated in the music. Boys and girls can keep time with the playing by moving their hands as if they were strumming the instrument.

3. Individuals try the instrument while the class sings. They must first get a firm feeling for the location of the two chord bars needed, playing them several times. The chords for the first songs are best learned by rote. To attempt to strum the strings, change the chord bars, *and* watch the music in the book all at once presents too many difficulties at one time. Cue the chord changes to words in the song thus:

G   G   G   G

I'm gonna sing when the spirit says, "sing" _____,

G   G D^7 D^7

I'm gonna sing when the spirit says, "sing" _____, etc.

Some children learn to do this through singing the words; others are helped by seeing the words on the chalkboard with the places for the chord changes marked as above.

4. Boys and girls are interested in trying both loud and soft picks and in finding songs suitable for each type of pick. Some children have excellent coordination and quickly acquire skill in playing the autoharp. It is important, however, to allow all who wish to play to do so. This means that it will be necessary to give them a chance to practice on the instrument. Some children overcome their shyness and learn to play only when they have a chance from time to time to practice alone, and to get their movements organized so that they feel comfortable with the instrument.

5. Songs with additional chords, major and minor, can be learned in the same way as suggested above. Songs that have a steady rhythmic movement are best until the children have developed considerable skill in playing. Most elementary school song books include information in the classified index of the songs best suited for autoharp accompaniments.

6. Boys and girls who are learning to sing chording parts to songs as was suggested on page 100, will enjoy using the autoharp with these activities. In a song such as the following one, the class is divided into two groups. While the autoharp is played, one group

sings the words and melody of the song and the other group sings the chord roots, changing notes whenever the autoharp chord changes. Syllables, numbers, letter names, or suitable words can be used for singing the chord roots.

ANIMAL SONG

Words and Music by
Emelyn E. Gardner

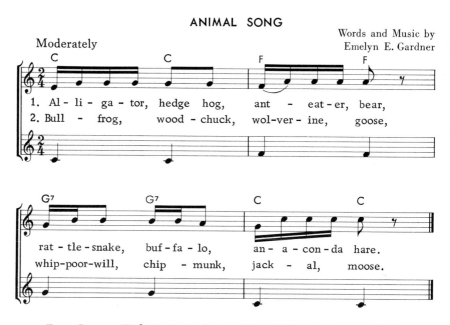

From *Growing With Music*, Book 4, p. 153. © 1966 by Prentice-Hall, Inc.

7. Some classes can sing not only the chord root, as they play the autoharp chords, but also one or two additional harmony parts, using the other voices of the chords. Singing these parts is possible in root position, but is often easier if inversions are used, so that the following chords might be used for the "Animal Song."

For this type of chording, it is best to have the chords sung with a sustained syllable or with the voices humming. Sometimes it is effective to have one or two voices alone sing the melody, supported by a tuned bar instrument or a recorder, while the other voices and the autoharp provide a soft accompaniment. When various instruments are used together in this way, it is important that they be in tune with each other.

8. Use the autoharp as a means of establishing the pitch and tempo of a song by having a few chords played as an introduction. For example, the "Animal Song" could have an introduction like this played at the speed the song is to be sung: C C G⁷ C.

9. A few boys and girls are usually able, with practice, to learn to play both melody and chords on the autoharp.

Sources on
the Use of the Autoharp
in the Classroom

Books

Barr, Lawrence, Elizabeth Blair, and Walter Ehret, *You and Music*, Englewood Cliffs, N. J.: Prentice-Hall, Inc., 1959.

Garretson, Robert L., *Music in Childhood Education*. New York: Appleton-Century-Crofts, 1966.

Gary, Charles L., ed., *The Study of Music in the Elementary School*. Washington, D.C.: Music Educators National Conferenece, 1967.

Hall, Frances, *How to Play the Autoharp*. Boston: The Boston Music Co., 1956.

Krone, Beatrice P., *Harmony Fun with the Autoharp*. Park Ridge, Ill.: Neil A. Kjos Music Company, Publisher, 1952.

————, and Kurt R. Miller, *Help Yourselves to Music* (2nd ed.). Belmont, Calif.: Wadsworth Publishing Company, Inc., 1968.

Ludwig, Alice J., and Louis Ludwig, *Colors and Chords*. Far Rockaway, N.Y.: Carl Van Roy Co.

McLaughlin, R., and Muriel Dawley, *Sing and Play with the Autoharp*. Far Rockaway, N.Y.: Carl Van Roy Co., 1958.

Nye, Robert E., and Vernice T. Nye, *Exploring Music with Children*. Belmont, Calif.: Wadsworth Publishing Company, Inc., 1966.

————, *Music in the Elementary School* (3rd ed.). Englewood Cliffs, N.J.: Prentice-Hall, Inc., 1970.

————, and Bjornar Bergethon, *Basic Music* (3rd ed.). Englewood Cliffs, N.J.: Prentice-Hall, Inc., 1968.

Pierce, Anne E., *Teaching Music in the Elementary School*. New York: Holt, Rinehart & Winston, Inc., 1959.

Slind, Lloyd H., and D. Evan Davis, *Bringing Music to Children*. New York: Harper & Row, Publishers, 1964.

Snyder, Alice M., *Sing and Strum*. New York: Mills Music Inc., 1957.

Swanson, Bessie R., *Music in the Education of Children* (3rd ed.). Belmont, Calif.: Wadsworth Publishing Company, Inc., 1969.

Elementary School Music Series

Every elementary school music series in use at the present time includes great numbers of songs that have the chords identified so that an autoharp accompaniment can easily be played. These begin with songs in the books for the very small children, where the autoharp would probably be played by the teacher. They continue throughout all levels, with suggestions for playing by the children themselves, first strumming while the teacher presses the bars, then playing the instrument independently when they are able. Some series include instructions for the children in their books; for example, "Playing Chords on an Autoharp," *Making Music Your Own*, Books 3, 4, and 5.

GAMBA
AND PSALTERY

The gamba and psaltery used for classroom music activities are smaller in size than the traditional instruments known by these names, and they are simplified in construction for playing by children. The gamba is included in some sets of Orff instruments. It is used more frequently in classes in European schools than in the United States. Parts for the gamba to play are included in many of the orchestrations in the Orff *Music for Children;* for example, "The Spider and the Fly" in *Book I, Pentatonic*. Some classes use the cello or string bass in place of the gamba since many of the gamba parts in the Orff books can be played on the open strings of these instruments.

The psaltery is a small stringed instrument that lies flat on the table like a zither or an autoharp. It is a diatonic instrument in key of C. Children use it for playing familiar melodies, and it is also especially valuable for their use in creating original melodies. Because of its very light tone, it can easily be used in a "Music Corner" in a classroom; the playing of the instrument by a child will not cause interference in a classroom where regular, non-music classroom activities are in progress. Parts for the psaltery to play are included with such songs as "See-Saw, Margery Daw" in *Music 'Round the Clock (Together We Sing*, Book 1).

THE UKULELE

The Hawaiian ukulele has musical value as a classroom instrument for children who are old enough to master the fingerings easily—usually beginning at the intermediate grade level. Besides providing a very enjoyable musical activity for both in-school and out-of-school participation, this little instrument can also motivate boys and girls to practice singing simple harmony parts by ear. Most of the songs best suited for ukulele accompaniments seem also suited to simple harmonization by voices.

The ukulele is a relatively inexpensive instrument and, while in the hands of an expert its chordal accompaniments can be very complex, in the hands of boys and girls a few simple chordal patterns will be sufficient to produce a very attractive accompaniment. Ukuleles made of wood and of plastic are available; those of wood have been found more durable in elementary school classes, since they do not break as easily as those of plastic. In the selection of a ukulele, the tuning pegs are important; if the instrument is to say in tune, tuning pegs with screws are more satisfactory than those that are simply inserted into holes.

Classroom Activities
with the Ukulele

1. The sound of the ukulele is not loud or heavy and therefore it is feasible for all boys and girls in a class to play together, if desired. However, even if there are only a few ukulele players, they can provide an interesting and suitable accompaniment for selected songs sung by the class. Many current school music books include ukulele chord symbols for some of the songs.

2. Since the ukulele has only four strings, it is reasonably easy to tune. Each player should learn from the beginning to tune his own instrument and to be constantly aware of the tuning. Many ukulele instruction books direct the player to tune his instrument to A-D-F#-B and with this tuning the easiest fingerings will be in keys of G major and D major. Some school books suggest tuning to G-C-E-A, providing easy fingerings for keys of F and C. Several books include both tunings, thus making it possible for the children to play songs easily in any of these four keys, but necessitating retuning from time to time according to the keys of the songs sung. For beginning groups it will be wise to select only one tuning and use it consistently until the players are comfortable playing the chords they are using. Later other chords or another tuning can be added.

3. It is recommended that songs using only one or two chords be used for the first playing experiences with the ukulele. These first songs should also be familiar enough so that the children can sing them from memory as they concentrate on playing the chords in the accompaniment. Here is such a song:

THE MORE WE GET TOGETHER

German Folk Song

The more we get to - geth-er, to - geth-er, to - geth-er;

The more we get to - geth-er, the hap-pier are we!

For your friends are my friends, and my friends are your friends,

The more we get to - geth - er, the hap-pier, are we!

From *Growing With Music,* Book 4, p. 81. © 1966 by Prentice-Hall, Inc.

The ukuleles will be tuned to G-C-E-A in order to play the two chords needed in this song.

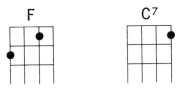

The children should be given an opportunity to practice the fingerings for the two chords until they can be played smoothly; then they can be used with the song. Most children, especially those who have played the autoharp, can quickly recognize by ear the places where the chords must be changed. If necessary, the teacher can signal the chord changes the first few times. When this song is easily played, other familiar songs in the same key and using the same chords can quickly be learned. In the classified index of most school music books, songs requiring only one or two chords for autoharp accompaniments are listed, and many of these can also be used with the ukulele.

4. Ukulele accompaniments are particularly well-suited for Hawaiian songs like this one. When the children are ready to learn a new chord, they may add this one, and sing and play the song

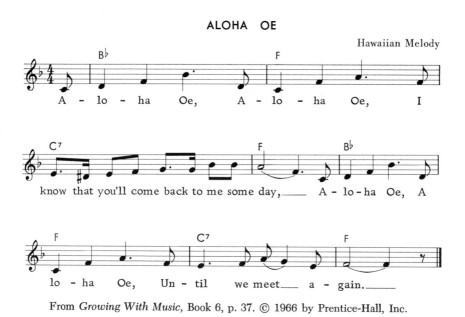

ALOHA OE

Hawaiian Melody

A - lo - ha   Oe,   A - lo - ha   Oe,   I

know that you'll come back to me some day,____ A - lo - ha Oe, A

lo - ha   Oe,   Un - til   we meet____ a - gain.____

From *Growing With Music,* Book 6, p. 37. © 1966 by Prentice-Hall, Inc.

5. The accompaniment furnished by the ukulele lends itself to vocal harmonizing by the class, by individuals, or by small groups. Frequently the harmonies are the traditional "barbershop" type, in which some singers add a simple part that is chiefly a third or a sixth above or below the melody. For example the song above, "Farewell to Thee," could be harmonized in barbershop style thus:

ALOHA OE

Hawaiian Melody

A - lo - ha Oe,   A - lo - ha Oe,   I

know that you'll come back to me some day ; ____ A - lo - ha Oe, A-

lo - ha Oe,   Un - til   we meet__ a - gain. ____

This type of harmonizing is well-suited to the needs of the boy whose voice is deepening and whose range may therefore be limited. The song above could, for example be sung with the same harmony part *below* the melody instead of above it. Learning to harmonize songs by ear in this way requires time, practice, and patience. First attempts are not always successful or musical, but the skill to sustain such a part can develop gradually and can provide a means of pleasurable informal singing activity. This can be done without ukulele accompaniment, of course, but somehow the playing of this type of instrument seems to encourage singers to experiment with vocal harmonization.

6. The playing of the ukulele adds appreciably to interest in units of study on Hawaiian life and history. The addition of suitable rhythm instruments to the ukulele accompaniment in playing native song and dance music will provide further possible experiences. (See page 83.)

**Sources on
the Use of the
Ukulele in the Classroom***

Books

Garretson, Robert L., *Music in Childhood Education.* New York: Appleton-Century-Crofts, 1966.

Gilmore, Lee, *Folk Instruments.* Minneapolis: Lerner Publications Co., 1962.

* Also see page 127 for listing of music for classroom ensembles.

Keen, Laura Johnson, *Sing and Play the Ukulele*. Far Rockaway, N.Y.: Carl Van Roy Co., 1957.

Nye, Robert E., and Vernice T. Nye, *Music in the Elementary School* (3rd ed.). Englewood Cliffs, N.J.: Prentice-Hall, Inc., 1970.

Slind, Lloyd H., and D. Evan Davis, *Bringing Music To Children*. New York: Harper & Row, Publishers, 1964.

Swanson, Bessie R., *Music in the Education of Children* (3rd ed.). Belmont, Calif.: Wadsworth Publishing Company, Inc., 1969.

Elementary Music Series Books

Songs with ukulele accompaniments: "Hawaiian Song," *Growing With Music*, Book 6; "My Boat," *This Is Music*, Book 4; "The Ukulele," *This Is Music*, Books 5, 6, 7, 8; "Feasting by the Ocean," *Discovering Music Together*, Book 5; "Teaching the Ukulele," *Making Music* (*Teacher's Guide, Music for Young Americans*, Book 5); "Aloha Oe," *Discovering Music Together*, Book 6; "Li'l Liza Jane," "That's Where My Money Goes," *Music for Young Americans*, Book 7; "Old Blue," *This Is Music*, Book 8.

THE GUITAR
AND THE MANDOLIN

The guitar and the mandolin are fretted instruments that play both melodies and chords. They are not commonly used in elementary schools, probably because of their size, their cost, and the fact that few teachers know enough about them to use them in teaching. Actually they can prove to be instruments of great value to elementary school music classes, contributing to the general learnings of the children in music and providing a unique avenue for out-of-school musical activity.

The guitar has six strings, tuned upward to E, A, D, G, B, and E.

A small-sized instrument is manufactured and is more feasible for use by children than the full-sized guitar. It is wise to allow a child plenty of time to practice each chord as it is learned, using much the same procedure as was suggested for piano chording on page 101, for autoharp, page 114, and for ukulele, page 119. A class can begin by learning a few chords in the key of C, and guitar accompaniments for many familiar songs like "Row, Row, Row Your Boat," "Skip to My Lou," and "Merrily We Roll Along" can be played in C using only these two chords:

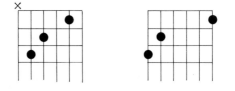

The "x" means that the player is not to strum the string so marked. A simplified way of playing chords is given in *The Guitar in the Classroom* listed below, and is extremely useful for beginning classes.

There is an increasing amount of interest in the use of the guitar in the schools as an accompanying instrument for folk music. Instructions for playing the instrument are given in several of the current school music series. In addition to its use in accompanying songs, the guitar can have great value in the classroom, especially if no piano is available for producing the low notes when children are learning to sing and play a chording bass to some of their songs (see page 99). The low pitches available on the instrument make it particularly suitable for this type of activity in classes where some of the voices are low. European school music teachers frequently use the guitar as a teaching tool, and parts for it are included in some of the Carl Orff books (see page 127).

The mandolin is seldom played in this country, but it is very important in the school music activities of Israel. It is used in that country not only as an instrument for accompanying informal singing, but also as an instrument for teaching the basic fundamentals of music and laying a foundation for the playing of standard stringed instruments. (The mandolin is tuned exactly like the violin, but has four double strings.) Large, well-balanced orchestras of mandolins of various sizes are to be found in the schools and also in Israeli community centers.

**Sources on
Guitar and Mandolin***

Books

Bay, Mel, *The Mel Bay Guitar Method.* Kirkwood, Mo.: Mel Bay Publications, 1960.

Gilmore, Lee, *Folk Instruments.* Minneapolis: Lerner Publications Company, 1962.

* Also see page 127 for listing of music for classroom ensembles.

The Guitar in the Classroom. Chicago: American Music Conference, 1967.

Moore, Jack, *Music for the Guitar.* Chicago: M. M. Cole Publishing Co., 1962.

Nye, Robert E., and Vernice T. Nye, *Music in the Elementary School* (3rd ed.). Englewood Cliffs, N.J.: Prentice-Hall, Inc., 1970.

Slind, Lloyd H., and D. Evan Davis, *Bringing Music To Children.* New York: Harper & Row, Publishers, 1964.

Elementary Music Series Books

Songs with guitar accompaniments: "Billy Boy," *Making Music Your Own,* Book 6; "Cindy," *Discovering Music Together,* Book 5; "The Colorado Trail," *Discovering Music Together,* Book 7; "Guitar," *This Is Music,* Books 7, 8; "Mingo Mountain," *Music in Our Country* (*Music for Living,* Book 5); "Trampin'," *Exploring Music, The Junior Book.*

USING ORCHESTRAL STRINGED INSTRUMENTS AS CLASSROOM INSTRUMENTS

Chording

Many elementary school classrooms include children who have already had basic instruction on the standard stringed instruments, violin, viola, cello, and bass viol. These instruments can also be used by boys and girls who have not played them before for playing simple chord root accompaniments to the songs the class sings, as was suggested on page 113. The notes for the chord roots are played by plucking the open strings of the instrument. The cello lends itself particularly to this kind of activity because of its pitch and the notes of its open strings, C-G-D-A. For example, it is possible to pluck a chord root accompaniment on the cello for any song that is harmonized by using only the chords on C and G. ("Intry Mintry" on page 99 could be used in this way.) In case a viola is available, the same type of accompaniment can be played on it since it is also tuned to C-G-D-A, but an octave higher than the cello. The violin (G-D-A-E) and the bass viol (E-A-D-G) can be used in the same way with songs that can be harmonized by chords using the chord roots available on the open strings of the instruments. Suggestions for chording parts using some of these instruments are given in many of the elementary school music books.

This type of activity provides great enjoyment to children, many of whom would never otherwise have an opportunity to hold a stringed instrument and produce a tone on it. The simple action of plucking open strings can give boys and girls their first exciting experience with such an instrument, and will sometimes be the means of motivating them to study one of the stringed instruments.

Playing an Ostinato

Ostinato parts included in some of the orchestrations in the Carl Orff *Music for Children* can sometimes be played by plucking open strings on these instruments, perhaps substituting them for parts originally written for gamba, bass, or timpani with only an occasional change in octave sequence. Most of the bass parts in the Orff orchestrations require notes that cannot be produced with the use of the open strings.

**Sources on
Using Orchestral
Stringed Instruments
as Classroom Instruments***

Books

Orff, Carl and Gunild Keetman, *Music for Children, I, Pentatonic.* English adaptation by Doreen Hall and Arnold Walter. Mainz, Germany: B. Schott's Söhne (USA, Associated Music Publishers, New York) 1960. "Mother May I Go and Bathe?"; "The Spider and the Fly"; "The Bells in the Steeple." From the same series, *Music for Children, II, Major Bordun,* "Nonsense Song." From *Music for Children, IV, Minor Bordun,* "Land of the Silver Birch."

Slind, Lloyd H., and D. Evan Davis, *Bringing Music to Children.* New York: Harper & Row, Publishers, 1964.

Swanson, Bessie R., *Music in the Education of Children* (3rd ed.). Belmont, Calif.: Wadsworth Publishing Company, Inc., 1969.

Elementary Music Series Books

Songs with chord root parts for orchestral stringed instruments: "The Darby Ram," "Zum Gali Gali," *This Is Music,* Book 5; "Sad Song," *Exploring Music,* Book 5, Teacher's Edition; "The 'Cello," "Blow the Wind Southerly," *Basic Goals in Music,* Book 5; "Twilight," *This Is Music,* Book 7; "On My Journey Home," "The Lone Prairie," *This Is Music,* Book 8; "The Fiddle," *Music Round the Town* (*Together We Sing,* Book 2).

* Also see page 127 for listing of music for classroom ensembles.

MUSIC FOR
ENSEMBLES OF
CLASSROOM INSTRUMENTS

Beckman, Frederick, *Music for Melody Instruments*. Philadelphia: Elkan-Vogel Co., 1952.

Bennett, Richard Rodney, *The Midnight Thief*. New York: Mills Music, Inc., 1963. Operetta for voices, tuned bar instruments, and rhythm instruments.

Bentley, Arnold, *Songs To Sing and Play*. London: Novello and Co., 1964. Recorder, tuned bar instruments, rhythm instruments.

Bergese, Hans, *Europe in Song*. Vols. 1–4. Wolfenbüttel, Germany: Möseler Verlag, 1963. Voices, recorders, tuned bar instruments, rhythm instruments.

Burakoff, Gerald, and Lawrence Wheeler, *Music Making in the Elementary School*. New York: Hargail Press, 1968. Voices, recorder, tuned bars, rhythm instruments.

Doolin, Howard A., *A New Introduction to Music*. Levels 1, 2, 3, and 4, including charts, easel books for students, and teacher's score manuals. Park Ridge, Ill.: General Words and Music Co., 1966, 1967, 1968. Tuned bar instruments, autoharp, voices, recorder, rhythm instruments, Melodica, string bass, piano.

Galloway, Margaret, *Carols for Singing and Playing*. New York: Oxford University Press, Inc., 1964. Tuned bar instruments, keyboard instruments, rhythm instruments, psaltery.

Golding, Sally, Eugene Lonstein, and Jerrold Ross, *Melodies for Music Makers*. Far Rockaway, N.Y.: Carl Van Roy Co., 1963. Small winds, tuned bar instruments, rhythm instruments.

Hoenack, Peg, *Let's Sing and Play Together*. Levels 1, 2, and 3 including charts, easel books for children, teacher's guide. Chevy Chase, Md.: Ellsworth Studios, 1965, 1967, 1968, 1969. Tuned bar instruments, small wind instruments, autoharp, guitar, piano.

Kendell, Iain, *Junior Music*. London: J. & W. Chester, Ltd., 1967 (USA: Edward B. Marks Music Corp., New York). Separate pieces for voices, recorder, tuned bar instruments, rhythm instruments, optional strings.

Marquis, Margaret H., *Songs for All Seasons and Rhymes without Reasons*. New York: Edward B. Marks Music Corp., 1968. Voices, tuned bar instruments, rhythm instruments.

McLaughlin, Roberta, and Muriel Dawley, *Make Music with the Bells*. Far Rockaway, N.Y.: Carl Van Roy Co., 1958. Voices, tuned bar instruments, rhythm instruments, autoharp.

Newman, Harold, *Music Shall Live*. New York: Hargail Music Press. Recorder, autoharp, guitar.

Orff, Carl, and Gunild Keetman, *Orff-Schulwerk, Music for Children*. English adaptation by Doreen Hall and Arnold Walter. Volumes (all 1960): I—*Pentatonic*; II—*Major Bordun*; III—*Major Triads*; IV—*Minor Bordun*; V—*Minor*

Triads. Voices, tuned bar instruments, rhythm instruments, strings, recorder. Also available: *Teacher's Manual,* Doreen Hall, 1961; *Eight Nursery Songs,* Margaret Murray, 1963; *Singing Games and Dances,* Doreen Hall, 1963; *Nursery Rhymes and Songs,* Doreen Hall, 1961. Mainz, Germany: B. Schott's Söhne (USA: Associated Music Publishers, New York). Recordings available: *Music for Children,* Carl Orff and Gunild Keetman, Angel-Capitol Records, B 3582; *Musica Poetica* (songs and chants in German), Harmonia Mundi Record Co., Münster, Germany (USA: Apon Records Co., New York).

Pendleton, Aline, and Edward Pendleton, *Reflets Folkloriques.* Paris: Editions Musicales, Alphonse Leduc, 1967. Voices, tuned bar instruments, rhythm instruments, recorder, cello, guitar.

Rees, Olive, *Sing With Chimes.* New York: Oxford University Press, Inc., 1963. Rhythm instruments and very easy tuned bar instrument parts.

————, and Anne Mendoza, *Carols With Chimes.* New York: Oxford University Press, Inc., 1965. Traditional carols for voices, tuned bar instruments, recorder, rhythm instruments.

————, *Songs and Tunes for Junior Ensembles.* New York: Oxford University Press, Inc., 1961. Voices, recorders, tuned bar instruments, rhythm instruments.

Rowen, Ruth, and Bill Simon, *Jolly Come Sing and Play.* New York: Carl Fischer, Inc., 1956. Songs with rhythm instruments, small winds, tuned bar instruments, chordal instruments.

Slind, Lloyd H., *Melody, Rhythm and Harmony for the Elementary Grades.* New York: Mills Music, Inc., 1953. Voices, small winds, autoharp, tuned bar instruments, rhythm instruments, orchestral stringed instruments, guitar, ukulele.

Staples, Rj., *Let's Play the Classroom Instruments.* Far Rockaway, N.Y.: Carl Van Roy Co., 1958. Separate parts for small winds, tuned bar instruments, rhythm instruments. Teacher's score.

Swift, Frederic Fay, *Together We Sing and Play.* New York: Edward B. Marks Music Corp., 1964. Part songs, strings, flute and recorder, autoharp, guitar and keyboard instruments.

Appendix

ELEMENTARY
SCHOOL MUSIC SERIES

Basic Goals in Music, Books 1–8. Lloyd H. Slind et al. McGraw-Hill Company of Canada, 1964–67.

Discovering Music Together. Charles Leonhard et al. Chicago: Follett Publishing Company. 1966–67. Books 1–8 plus teachers' editions, charts, and recordings.

Exploring Music. Eunice Boardman et al. New York: Holt, Rinehart & Winston, Inc., 1966–68. Books K–8 plus teachers' editions and recordings.

Growing With Music. Harry R. Wilson et al. Englewood Cliffs, N.J.: Prentice-Hall, Inc., 1963–66. Books K–8 plus teachers' editions and recordings.

The Magic of Music. Lorrain E. Watters et al. Boston: Ginn and Company, 1965–68. Books K–6 plus teachers' editions and recordings.

Making Music Your Own. Harold C. Youngberg et al. Morristown, N.J.: Silver Burdett Company, 1964–68. Books 1–8 plus teachers' editions and recordings.

Music for Young Americans (2nd ed.). Richard C. Berg et al. New York: American Book Company, 1966. Books K–6 plus teachers' editions and recordings. Books 7–8, 1961.

This Is Music (2nd ed.). William R. Sur et al. Boston: Allyn and Bacon, Inc. K–8 plus teachers' editions, accompaniment books, recordings and charts, 1967.

ADDRESSES
OF PUBLISHERS

Allyn & Bacon, Inc., 150 Tremont St., Boston, Mass.

American Book Company, 55 Fifth Ave., New York, N.Y.

American Music Conference, 332 South Michigan Ave., Chicago, Ill.

Ann Arbor Publishers, 611 Church St., Ann Arbor, Mich.

Appleton-Century-Crofts, 440 Park Ave. South, New York, N.Y.

Associated Music Publishers, One West 47th St., New York, N.Y.

Mel Bay Publications, Kirkwood, Mo.

Boosey & Hawkes, Inc., Oceanside, N.Y.

The Boston Music Company, 116 Boylston St., Boston, Mass.

Bowmar Publishing Corp., 622 Radier Dr., Glendale, Calif.

Wm. C. Brown Company, Publishers, 135 So. Locust St., Dubuque, Ia.

J. and W. Chester, London (USA: Edward B. Marks Music Corp., 136 W. 52nd St., New York, N.Y.).

Children's Music Center, Inc., 5373 West Pico Blvd., Los Angeles, Calif.

M. M. Cole Publishing Co., 823 S. Wabash Ave., Chicago, Ill.

Cooperative Recreation Service, Delaware, O.

The John Day Company, Inc., 200 Madison Ave., New York, N.Y.

E. P. Dutton & Co., Inc., 201 Park Ave. South, New York, N.Y.

Elkan-Vogel Co., 1716 Sansom St., Philadelphia, Pa.

Ellsworth Studios, 4611 Willow Lane, Chevy Chase, Md.

Carl Fischer, Inc., 62 Cooper Square, New York, N.Y.

Follett Publishing Company, 1010 W. Washington Blvd., Chicago, Ill.

General Words and Music Co., 525 Busse Highway, Park Ridge, Ill.

Ginn and Company, Statler Bldg., Boston, Mass.

H. W. Gray Co., Inc., 159 E. 48th St., New York, N.Y.

Grossman Company, 740 Bolivar Road, Cleveland, Ohio.

Hargail Music Press, 130 W. 56th St., New York, N.Y.

Harper & Row, Publishers, 49 E. 33rd St., New York, N.Y.

Hillsdale Educational Publishers, Hillsdale, Mich.

Holt, Rinehart & Winston, Inc., 383 Madison Ave., New York, N.Y.

International Communication Films, 1371 Reynolds Ave., Santa Ana, Calif.

Dorothy M. Kahanaui, University of Hawaii, Honolulu, Hawaii.

Neil A. Kjos Music Company, Publisher, 525 Busse Highway, Park Ridge, Ill.

Lerner Publications, 241 First Ave. North, Minneapolis, Minn.

Lyons Band Instrument Co., 688 Industrial Dr., Elmhurst, Ill.

Edward B. Marks Music Corporation, 136 W. 52nd St., New York, N.Y.

McGraw-Hill Book Company, 330 W. 42nd St., New York, N.Y.

McGraw-Hill Company of Canada, 330 Progress Ave., Scarborough, Ont.

David McKay Co., Inc., 750 Third Ave., New York, N.Y.

Melody Flute Co., Laurel, Md.

Mills Music, Inc., 1619 Broadway, New York, N.Y.

Antonio J. Molina, Manila, The Philippines.

Möseler Verlag, Wolfenbüttel, Germany.

Music Educators National Conference, 1201–16th St., N.W., Washington, D.C.

W. W. Norton & Company, Inc., 55 Fifth Ave., New York, N.Y.

Novello and Co., Ltd., London (USA: H. W. Gray Co., Inc.).

Oxford University Press, Inc., 417 Fifth Ave., New York, N.Y.

Edizioni Pegasis, Locarno, Switzerland (USA: C. F. Peters Corp.).

C. F. Peters Corp., 373 Park Ave. South, New York, N.Y.

Plymouth Music Co., Inc., 1841 Broadway, New York, N.Y.

Prentice-Hall, Inc., Englewood Cliffs, N.J.

Theodore Presser Company, Bryn Mawr, Penna.

G. P. Putnam's Sons, 200 Madison Ave., New York, N.Y.

Rhythm Band, Inc., P.O. Box 126, Fort Worth, Texas.

St. Martin's Press, Inc., 175 Fifth Ave., New York, N.Y.

G. Schirmer, Inc., 609 Fifth Ave., New York, N.Y.

Schott, Publishers, London (USA: Associated Music Publishers).

B. Schotts Söhne, Mainz, Germany (USA: Associated Music Publishers).

Scott, Foresman & Co., 1900 East Lake Ave., Glenview, Ill.

Silver Burdett Company, Morristown, N.J.

Sterling Publishing Co., Inc., 419–4th Ave., New York, N.Y.

Trophy Products Co., Cleveland, O.

E. Tuttle Co., Rutland, Vt.

U.S. Text Book Co., Putnam, Conn.

Carl Van Roy Co., 51–17 Rockaway Beach Blvd., Far Rockaway, N.Y.

Wadsworth Publishing Company, Inc., Belmont, Calif.

Franklin Watts, 575 Lexington Ave., New York, N.Y.

Willis Music Co., 440 Main St., Cincinnati, O.

M. Witmark and Sons (Music Publishers Holding Corp.), 488 Madison Ave., New York, N.Y.

Indexes

Index

Index of Songs

Index
of Instruments